Anglo-Saxon Verse Charms & Heroic Legends

Louis J Rodrigues

Anglo-Saxon Books

First Published 1993
Reprinted 1994

Published by
Anglo-Saxon Books
25 Malpas Drive
Pinner
Middlesex
England

Printed by
Antony Rowe Ltd.
Chippenham
Wiltshire
England

ISBN 1–898281–01–7

PREFACE

This fifth book in my series of **Anglo-Saxon Verse Specimens rendered into Modern English**, like its predecessors, is aimed at a non-academic audience. Had it been my intention to do otherwise, it should not have lacked a complete critical apparatus – the 'almost obligatory' variant editorial readings of the texts, a description of their linguistic characteristics, a glossary, a comprehensive bibliography, and perhaps yet another 'declaration of intent' to add to the existing chaos of genuine and spurious ones. I make this point merely to scotch the enthusiasm of 'pseudo-academic' reviewers into whose hands this book is likely to fall whose assertions by implication are usually that they could have done better themselves, which I have no reason to dispute. It would, also, do me no harm to reiterate that I prefer the terms 'Anglo-Saxon' to 'Old English' and 'render' to 'translate' for the reason that these fairly represent the compromise I feel must be effected between historical fact and simple reality. The original form of the language is after all sufficiently remote from modern usage in its orthography, syntax, and even its vocabulary, to be considered necessary to 'translate'; although, for the very reason that it is the historical predecessor of Modern English, one would expect, instead, to have it 'rendered' out of its 'antique' state into its 'modern' equivalent. I use the latter term advisedly to mean 'the language of the modern period' and not that of the twentieth century. In an effort, also, to maintain the atmosphere of the original, I have deliberately retained such Anglo-Saxon lexical items as have survived into this 'modern' period as I felt obliged to, at the same time as I have generally eschewed the involuted syntax of the texts, except in those cases where such an intrusion on my part into the realm of composition of the Anglo-Saxon *scop* would have spoilt the symmetry he had intended to impose on their structure.

LJR, Cambridge 1993

CONTENTS

INTRODUCTION

Just under thirty thousand lines is all that is now extant of what must have once been a considerable body of Anglo-Saxon verse, most of it in manuscripts of the late tenth or early eleventh centuries, of which slightly more than twenty thousand lines alone are to be found in four codices: the **Junius Manuscript**, the **Vercelli Book**, the **Exeter Book**, and the **Beowulf Manuscript**. The exact number of others that might have survived but for the Viking invasions that began in 793 is a matter of speculation. Only the **Exeter Book, the Beowulf Manuscript**, and a few other manuscripts that contain (or did contain) poems dealing with the heroic and folk traditions familiar to our Continental Anglo-Saxon ancestors before they decided to settle permanently in Britain are what concern us here.

The manuscripts are as follows:

(i)   MS Cotton Vitellius A xv, in the British Museum, for the 'Tales' of Sigemund, Finn, Thryth, and Freawuru, and the Battle of Ravenswood and Death of Ongentheow, in *Beowulf*;

(ii) MS 487 (now lost), in the Lambeth Palace Library, London, for the *Finnsburh Fragment.*

(iii) MS Ny kongelige Samling 167b, in the Royal Library, Copenhagen, for *Waldere.*

(iv) The Exeter Book, in the Chapter Library of Exeter Cathedral, for *Widsith, Deor, Wulf and Eadwacer*, and *Maxims I*;

(v)   MS Cotton Tiberius B i, in the British Museum, for *Maxims II*;

(vi) MS Cotton Caligula A vii, in the British Museum, for Charm 1, 'For Unfruitful Land';

(vii) MS Harley 585, in the British Museum, for Charms 2, 'The Nine Herbs Charm'; 3, 'Against a Dwarf'; 4, 'For a Sudden Stitch'; 5, 'For Loss of Cattle'; and 6, 'For Delayed Birth';

(viii) MS Royal 12D xvii, in the British Museum, for Charm 7, 'For the Water-elf Disease';

(ix) MS 41, in the Library of Corpus Christi College, Cambridge, for Charms 8, 'For a Swarm of Bees'; 9, 'For Theft of Cattle'; 10, 'For Loss of Cattle'; and 11, 'A Journey Charm;

(x)   MS Royal 4A xiv, in the British Museum, for Charm 12, 'Against a Wen'.

(A) HEROIC TRADITION

Although the earliest extant Anglo-Saxon specimens of Germanic heroic verse indicate that their authors and audiences were already influenced by Christianity, they preserve much of the culture that Tacitus describes in his *Germania*, an account of the Germanic tribes written towards the close of the first century, that extols the basic Germanic values enshrined in what was known as the *comitatus* bond – loyalty to chosen aristocratic chieftains even to death and beyond, the sacredness of the ties of kinship, the supreme duty of avenging a slain leader, and a deep devotion of a type of naturalistic religion whose heroic leaders were derived from the gods through carefully remembered genealogies. It is from the *Germania* that we first learn of these ancient Germanic heroic lays, *carmina antiqua* – from which the earliest strata of Anglo-Saxon verse are ultimately derived. In his third chapter, Tacitus tells us that these lays are the sole means of ('oral') transmission of the tribal historical and legendary traditions; and that they record how the hero-god, 'bravest of all men', Herakles, whom he calls by the Roman name Hercules, was once among them. They celebrate in ancient lays, he says, the founder of the whole Germanic race Tuisto, their principal deity and founder, who has sprung from the earth. As they are about to go into battle, he tells us in the same chapter, the Germani, singing war-songs of Hercules, chant a kind of declamation or war-cry which they term by a probably onomatopoeic word Latinized as *barritus*. This *barritus* inflames the minds of the warriors to war; and by its varying tones the fortunes of the impending battle may be discovered by divination. In this recitation, 'harshness of sound and a kind of rhythmic rising and falling are especially aimed at, as the sound of the voices is made to swell out more fully and with more powerful weight through the repercussion caused by placing men's shields in front of their faces.' Just as we have it in *Beowulf*, at a banquet given by the king or leader to his noble retainers or *comitatus*, the Anglo-Saxon *scop* recited in the great hall while the warriors feasted. It is the way in which they share to a varying extent in these Continental traditions of the heroic history and legend from the migration periods of the fourth, fifth, and sixth centuries that gives a certain community of tone to the otherwise somewhat heterogeneous group of short poems that follow our initial examination of the series of 'Tales' in *Beowulf* below. They are what remains, in fragmentary and allusively incomplete form, of material from Germanic heroic story which the Angles, Saxons, and

Jutes must have brought to Britain from their homelands, with an already established tradition of metre, diction, and style. But this material and the outlook in which it is expressed is properly to be regarded as Germanic rather than Anglo-Saxon. For the Germanic peoples had thought of themselves as based upon the idea of the clan, not in any sense of nationality. Even as late as *Beowulf*, in which the characters of the stories which make up the poem are of differing Germanic tribes –Danes, Geats, Swedes– the outlook is still mainly Continental Germanic, though fundamentally touched by Christian culture.

BEOWULF

One important repository of Continental traditions surviving into the period of composition of Anglo-Saxon verse is *Beowulf*, an epic poem which probably evolved in Anglian territory, either in Bede's Northumbria or in Offa's Mercia. It is a composite of traditional Germanic material of history, legend, and folklore that came to be Christianized in an Anglo-Saxon cultural environment. Though some of this material was probably known from traditional lays, the poem's structure evidences a deliberate and highly developed art in which its variety of episodes and digressions, alien to the epic traditions of Greece and Rome, vividly enhances and heightens the poetic effectiveness of its simple central narratives. In subject-matter it is basically Germanic, even though its tone is characteristic of the peak of Anglo-Saxon civilization and there are two, possibly three, personages closely connected with Britain. These are Offa, the ancestor of Offa the Great of Mercia (757–96), Hengest the Jute, an embodiment of the traditions concerning the historical Hengest who led the Germanic invaders of the middle of the fifth century, and Finn (mentioned also in *Widsith*), whose name occurs in the Anglian genealogies. This last may possibly be linked with the leader in the 'Tale of Finn' of this poem and of the *Finnsburh Fragment*.

The modern reader may consider the plot of *Beowulf* far too trivial to rank as a great epic – since it is no more than a simple, disjointed tale of conflicts between its hero and supernatural monsters of evil. For, in his youth, Beowulf slays two of them, Grendel and his mother; and then, after fifty years of noble rule over the Geats, he is called upon to face a fire-breathing dragon which is laying waste his country. He slays it with the help of Wiglaf, a faithful retainer, but himself dies, exulting in his heroic past life and in the worthy memory he will leave posterity, just as Byrhtnoth of Essex does in the tenth century historical poem of the *Battle of Maldon* – both, examples of the Anglo-Saxon heroic spirit attaining its height in the moment of final confrontation with impossible odds.

Though most of its characters, including that of Beowulf himself, appear to belong to that traditional Germanic heroic material which is often inseparable from legend or mythology, the poem does contain elements of authentic and verifiable history. Hygelac, the King of the Geats, in Sweden, who is Beowulf's kinsman and lord, is mentioned in authentic historical writings which show him to have rashly invaded the territory of the Franks and Frisians about the year 520, and so met his death – an event which, according to this poem, led ultimately to Beowulf's succession to the throne. This great disaster to the Geats, repeatedly referred to allusively (1202 ff., 2363 ff., 2910 ff.) is used by the poet subtly and admirably in his creation of tragic atmosphere. Such external evidence of the date of the historic Hygelac makes it clear that the events of the poem, in so far as they can be considered factual, occurred in the latter half of the fifth century. The Geats themselves are known to history: and that they, along with the Swedes and the Danes, were of particular interest to the Anglo-Saxon aristocracy is suggested by their mention together in *Widsith*, where the protagonist claims to have been 'with the Swedes, the Geats and the South-Danes'(58). There is, again, the reference (1201) to the late fourth-century Gothic ruler Eormanric, notorious elsewhere in Germanic tradition, who appears also in *Deor* (21). The Sutton Hoo finds of armour and weapons of Swedish workmanship may also indicate Anglo-Saxon royal interest in Scandinavian ancestry. The wars of the Geats and Swedes which occupy much of the second part of *Beowulf*, and which probably had some special appeal to the poet and his audience, also reveal names and events authenticated by some external historical evidence. Most scholars believe that the Continental Germanic material in *Beowulf* was brought over by the Anglo-Saxon invaders, though the poem as a whole, with its Christian implications, could scarcely have been composed before the beginning of the eighth century.

Such material, as we have already observed, is presented in the form of numerous episodes and digressions, the distinction being that, an episode may be considered as a moment which forms a real whole and yet is merged in the main narrative, whereas a digression is more of an adjunction and generally entails a sudden break in the narrative. So, the 'Tale of Finn' may be considered to be a genuine type of episode since that part of legend as recited by the *scop* at the royal court is complete in itself; as a specimen of what he would sing on such occasions, it is part of the description of the festivities in Heorot. On the other hand, the 'Tale of Thryth' (introduced with reference to the young Geatish queen) is of the nature of a digression, since it rather abruptly interrupts the narration of Beowulf's return. This distinction, however, is not absolute as the word 'episode' is used in a very restricted sense by some critics whereas others consider 'episode' and 'digression' as synonymous. Each of the 'Tales' that follow is first placed in its proper context within the narrative framework of the poem and then examined at some length for the light it sheds on a heroic tradition with which the poet was familiar.

'The Tale of Sigemund' [874b–97]

On their way back to Heorot, the *scop* improvises a lay in honour of Beowulf and compares him to Sigemund and Heremod. He mentions Sigemund's fights against the giants (undertaken together with his nephew Fitela) and his successful dragon fight. Indeed, Sigemund was the most famous warrior since Heremod's death. The latter, though he had raised great expectations, became cruel and tyrannous and was hated by his people, whereas everyone loves Beowulf.

In its cursory, epitomizing form, this 'Tale' embodies two separate stories going back, possibly, to two originally distinct lays: (i) Sigemund's *wide siðas* of fierce fighting, especially those undertaken in company with Fitela, and (ii) his dragon fight.

According to the *Vǫlsungasaga* (chapters 3–8), Sigmundr is the eldest son of King Vǫlsungr, a descendant of Oþinn. Sigmundr's twin sister, Signý, is married against her will to Siggeirr, king of Gautland. While on a visit at Siggeirr's court, Vǫlsungr and his men are treacherously slain; his sons are captured and killed one after another except Sigmundr, who escapes into the forest. Sigmundr and Signý brood revenge. Seeing that her sons by Siggeirr are lacking in valour and that only a true Vǫlsung son will be able to help in the work of revenge, Signý, impelled by a desperate resolve, disguises herself as a witch and visits her brother in the forest. When her time comes, she gives birth to a son, who is named Sinfjǫtli. At his mother's bidding, when he is ten years old, the boy joins Sigmundr (who does not know until the final catastrophe that Sinfjǫtli is his son) and is trained by him in deeds of strength and endurance. Finally Sigmundr and Sinfjǫtli together accomplish the revenge by setting fire to Siggeirr's hall. How far the version

11

known to the author of *Beowulf* agreed with this part of the *Vǫlsungasaga*, it is impossible to determine. The fact that Fitela is referred to as Sigemund's *nefa* only (881), might perhaps be held to indicate Sigemund's own ignorance of their true relationship, or it may be attributed to the Christian author's desire to suppress what was considered a morally revolting motive. But we do not know, indeed, whether the Anglo-Saxons of that time were at all acquainted with the story answering to the Sigmundr-Signý motif. The form *Fitela* differs from the established Norse compound name *Sinfjǫtli* and from the High German *Sintarfizzilo*. Also, the designation of Sigemund's father as *Wæls* (897) differs from his Norse name *Vǫlsungr*, which latter is presumably the result of confusion, the patronymic form being taken for a proper name.

Sigemund's dragon fight is peculiar to *Beowulf*. It naturally suggests the famous dragon fight of his still greater son (Old Norse *Sigurðr*, Middle High German *Sigfrit*) which roused the imagination of the Scandinavians and was not forgotten by the Germans, and which in fact –especially as part of the great *Nibelungen* cycle– has been celebrated in modern Germanic epic, drama, and music. But there are differences between the two stories, quite apart from the greater fullness of detail found in the narrative of Sigurðr's exploit. The manner of the fight itself is not the same, Sigemund's deed appearing the more genuinely heroic one. Noteworthy incidents of the *Beowulf* version are the dissolving of the dragon in its own heat (897) and the carrying away of the hoard in a boat (895). It is widely held that the dragon fight belongs properly to Sigfrit and not to Sigemund, his father, yet there is no positive evidence to prove that the Anglo-Saxon poet was wrong when he attributed that exploit to the latter. Sigurðr-Sigfrit may, in fact, have been unknown to him. It is, on the whole, probable that in his allusions to Sigemund, as well as to Heremod, he followed Danish tradition, and that no connexion had yet been established between the Sigemund (*Wælsing*) legends and those of Sigfrit and of the Burgundians.

'The Tale of Finn' [1066b–1159a]

In the course of a brilliant ceremony at Heorot in honour of Beowulf's victory, the hero has been offered rich presents by the King. The festivities are carried on and then the scop recites the 'Tale of Finn' which is about a band of sixty Danes under their chief Hnæf who find themselves attacked before daybreak in the hall of the Frisian King Finn, whom they have come to visit . . . Five days they fight without loss against the Frisians, but at the end Hnæf and many of his men, as well as of the Frisians, are slain. Finn is forced to conclude a treaty with Hengest, who has now assumed command over the Danes. The fallen warriors of both tribes are burned together amid appropriate ceremonies and Hengest and his men remain in Friesland during the winter. Deep in his heart, however, Hengest yearns for revenge. The day of reckoning comes when the Danes Guthlaf and Oslaf, unable any longer to keep the silence imposed upon them by the terms of the treaty, openly rebuke their old foes. Finn is attacked and slain, and his queen, Hildeburh, together with the royal treasure of the Frisians, is carried back to the land of the Danes.

This 'Tale' is twice alluded to in *Beowulf* (in some detail, 1069 ff., and only briefly, 1151 ff.). For a resolution of some of the obscurities of the Finn Legend we must turn, however, to the *Finnsburh Fragment*, as it is obvious that the latter poem not only describes the events connected with the 'Tale' but also precedes it (see below for a fuller treatment of both versions). The antecedents to the conflict are lost to us. But evidently Hildeburh is in some way connected with the hostility between her brother and her husband. There may have existed an old feud between the two tribes, and the Danish princess had been given in marriage to the Frisian king in the hope of securing permanent peace, but with the same grievous result as in the case of Freawaru. Or the ill feeling may have dated from the wedding feast (as in the *Vǫlsungasaga*, chapter 3). It is possible also –though far from probable– that Hildeburh had been abducted like Hildr, Hogni's daughter, in Snorri's *Edda* and Hilde, Hagene's daughter in the Middle High German epic of *Kudrun*. At any rate, at least fifteen or twenty years must have elapsed after the marriage, since Hildeburh's son falls in the battle (1074, 1115).

'The Tale of Thryth' [1931b–62]
Beowulf returns to Geatland with his comrades. They have landed safely and are on their way to the royal hall where Hygelac resides with his young wife Hygd. Though she has not reigned long, she has proved a generous queen. (Mod)thrytho –and here the digression abruptly begins– perpetrated terrible deeds. No man dared look at her for fear of being put to death immediately. 'Ne bið swylc cwenlic þeaw idese to efnanne,' the poet says. On her father's bidding, she had sailed to the court of Offa and no sooner had she married him than she gave up her violent ways, and became a generous queen at Offa's side, who was himself a brave and excellent ruler. They had a son called Eomer.

Despite her youth, Hygd, Hrothgar's wife, shows the virtues of a discreet woman and a gracious, generous queen, differing thus from Thryth in her early pre-marital stage; and, in his 'Tale of Thryth', the *scop* probably intends this remarkable woman to represent a haughty, violent maiden, who cruelly has any man put to death who is bold enough merely to look at her fair face (1941), but who, after being wedded to the right husband, becomes an admirable, womanly wife (and kind, generous [1952] queen).

Offa, who while still young (1948) married the noble (1949), impetuous maiden, is extolled (1955 ff.) as the most excellent hero, famed for his valour, wisdom, and liberality. He is the son of Garmund and the father of Eomer, and corresponds to the legendary, pre-historic king of Angeln, Offa I of the Mercian genealogies. Being removed twelve generations from the historical Offa II, the old Angeln Offa may be assigned to the latter half of the fourth century. His great exploit is the single combat by the river Eider alluded to in *Widsith* (35 ff.).

The stories concerning both Offa and Thryth undoubtedly arose in the ancient continental home of the Angles. The Offa tradition lived on for centuries among the Danes, and it appears in literary, nationalized form (Warmundus figuring as the king of Denmark) in the pages of Saxo Grammaticus and Sven Aageson. On the other hand, the Angles migrating to Britain carried the legends of Offa and his queen with them and in course of time localized them in their new home. Offa I became in the *Vita* king of the West Angles (Mercians), the founder of the city of Warwick, and considerable confusion between the two Offas set in, leading to further variations.

'The Tale of Freawaru' [2024b–69a]

In his report to Hygelac Beowulf describes his reception at Heorot and alludes to the king's daughter Freawaru, who distributed the ale-cups to the *duguðe*.

The young princess is betrothed to Frotha's son, Ingeld, in an effort to put an end to the interminable feud between Danes and Heathobards. Beowulf warns that such a settlement is bound to be transient: the followers of Freawaru will carry swords that once belonged to Heathobard warriors who had been killed in battle (by the Danes), and the Heathobards will resent it. Then, 'an aged spearsman, who eyes a ring-hilt, remembers it all, the spear-death of heroes' (2041–3). He incites a young comrade, whose father's sword is now borne by a Dane in the Heathobards' hall, to an act of revenge. Again and again he spurs him on with bitter words until the young man kills Freawaru's thane. Retaliation will follow on the part of the Danes and this will kindle Ingeld's *wælniðas* whereas his love for his wife will grow cold. Therefore, Beowulf concludes, 'I hold hollow the Heathobards' lordly alliance with loyal Danes, a specious friendship' (2067–9).

Saxo's version of the Heathobard episode and the 'Tale of Freawaru' is as follows[1]. Frotho, who succeeded to the Danish throne when he was in his twelfth year, overcame and subjected the Saxon kings Swerting and Hanef. He proved an excellent king, strong in war, generous, virtuous, and honourable. Meanwhile Swerting, anxious to throw off the Danish yoke, treacherously resolved to slay Frotho, who forestalled and slew him, but was slain by him simultaneously. Frotho was succeeded by his son Ingellus, whose soul was perverted from honour. Forsaking the examples of his forefathers, he indulged in wanton profligacy. He married the daughter of Swerting given him by her brothers, who desired to insure themselves against the Danish king's vengeance. When Starcatherus, the former guardian of Frotho's son, heard that Ingellus was perversely minded, and instead of punishing his father's murderers, bestowed kindness and friendship upon them, he was vexed with stinging wrath at the heinousness of the crime. He returned from his wanderings in foreign lands, where he had been fighting, and clad in mean attire, betook himself to the royal hall and awaited the king. In the evening, Ingellus took his meal with the sons of Swerting, and enjoyed a magnificent feast. The tables had been loaded with the profusest dishes. The stern guest soon recognized by the king, violently spurned the queen's efforts to please him, and when he saw that Frotho's slayers were in high favour with the king, he could not refrain from attacking Ingellus's character, but poured out the whole bitterness of his reproaches on his head, to which he added a song that so roused Ingellus by its earnest admonition that he leapt up, drew his sword, and straightway slew the sons of Swerting.

Compared with the *Beowulf*, Saxo's version marks an advance in dramatic power in that the climax is brought about by a single act (not by exhortations made on several occasions, *mæla gehwylce* 2057), and that

---

[1] Saxo Grammaticus: Gesta Danorum, trans. O Elton (London, 1894), bk. vi, 182 ff.

Ingellus himself carries out the vengeance, whereas in the Anglo-Saxon poem the slaying of one of the queen's retinue by an unnamed warrior provokes the catastrophe.

'The Battle of Ravenswood & Death of Ongentheow' [2922–98]

Wiglaf's messenger predicts troublesome days ahead for the Geats when the Franks and Frisians hear of Beowulf's death. Neither are the Swedes to be trusted. He then refers to the Geatish invasion of Sweden (under Hæthcyn and Hygelac). Such was the origin of the feud and the enmity which the Swedes are –so the messenger says– likely to remember when they hear that Beowulf is dead.

The 'Battle of Ravenswood and Death of Ongentheow', belong to the history of the Geats and Swedes. Hrethel, like his contemporary Healfdene the Dane, has three sons and one daughter. The eldest son Herebeald is accidentally killed by Hæthcyn, who, when shooting an arrow, misses his aim and strikes his brother instead (2435 ff.). The grief caused by this tragic fate that has to go unavenged eats away at the king's life. Upon his death and the succession of Hæthcyn, war breaks out between the Geats and Swedes (2472 ff., 2922 ff.). It is started by the Swedes, who attack their southern neighbours and after inflicting severe damage return home. A punitive expedition into the land of the Swedes led by Hæthcyn and Hygelac, though initially successful (even Ongentheow's queen is taken prisoner), seems destined to utter failure; the 'aged and awesome' (2929) king of the Swedes falls upon Hæthcyn's army, rescues the queen, kills the Geat king and forces his troops to seek refuge in the woods (*Hrefnesholt* 2935), threatening them all night long with death in the morning by the sword and the gallows. But at dawn the valorous Hygelac appears with his division and inspires such a terror that the Swedes flee to their fastness, pursued by the Geats. Ongentheow in a brave fight against two brothers, Eofor and Wulf, loses his life. Hygelac, now king of the Geats, on his homecoming richly repays the brothers and gives his only daughter as wife to Eofor.

This victory at Ravenswood in the year 510 ensured the Geats peace with the Swedes, who seem to have dreaded the power of the warlike Hygelac.

Of the group of fragmentary short poems whose inspiration may be traced to the same source as *Beowulf*, there are five such of varying date, character, and homogeneity, comprising the *Finnsburh Fragment, Waldere, Widsith,*

Deor, and *Wulf and Eadwacer*. Two of these, the *Finnsburh Fragment* and *Waldere*, each found on odd sheets of parchment, are of approximately the same date in their extant forms as the other three, *Widsith, Deor*, and *Wulf and Eadwacer*, in the **Exeter Book**, an anthology of short, mostly lyric, poems copied at the close of the tenth century. Yet there is considerable disparity in their probable dates of origin. Moreover, their heroes came originally from different Germanic peoples, and none of them are in fact Anglo-Saxon. Nor, for the most part, did they originate from the Anglo-Saxon homelands. Finn, in the *Finnsburh Fragment*, was a Jutish king of the Frisians, though Hengest may be identified with the Hengest who led the invasion of Britain in English historical tradition. The Guthhere of *Waldere* is probably the king of the Burgundians better known as Gunther. Welund, the magic smith of *Deor*, was of South German origin, while Eormanric and Theodoric were Goths. But the protagonists of *Wulf and Eadwacer* are of no known provenance. Some of these characters of course, such as Welund, Eormanric, Finn, and Hengest, are also to be found in *Beowulf*. It is worth noting that both the *Finnsburh Fragment* and *Waldere* are short, incomplete poems whose tone and background are much more characteristic of Germanic heroic traditions, with their emphasis on war and the obligations of the Germanic *comitatus*, loyalty and the blood-feud (as described by Tacitus in his *Germania*). Both are portions of longer poems: *Waldere* of a probably epic poem of considerable length, and the *Finnsburh Fragment* of a heroic lay. Both, with an approach older than *Beowulf*, show something of the delight of battle, with plenty of simple vivid speeches of warlike boasting: but the *Finnsburh Fragment* is too short and incomplete to show much literary quality. The eighty lines in two disparate fragments of *Waldere*, and the forty-eight of the *Finnsburh Fragment*, are the most spirited and dramatic expression of tragic conflict that have survived in Anglo-Saxon from material of the ancient Germanic world.

THE FINNSBURH FRAGMENT

The only source of this fragment of forty-eight lines is George Hickes' copy of a single isolated folio which he found in a volume of homilies probably of the thirteenth century, in the Archbishop of Canterbury's London palace at Lambeth, and published in 1705 in his *Thesaurus*[2]. This somewhat free

---

2 Hickes, G: Linguarum Veterum Septentrionalium Thesaurus (Oxford, 1705), vol. i, pp. 192 ff.

transcription by Hickes has never been traced, so that his printed version remains its sole authoritative source. The text, as it stands, replete with Hickes' own errors, appears to date from the eleventh century. It was evidently part of a lay, of which the *Fragment* occurred near the beginning, while another version of a later portion occurs as an episodic lay recited by King Hrothgar's *scop* in *Beowulf* (1068–1159). A most vivid and dramatic poem treating of a tragic feud between Danes and Frisians, in which the leader of the Frisians was Finn, centred on Finn's fortified dwelling Finnsburh, this heroic piece is now usually printed as an appendix in editions of *Beowulf*.

The story in outline is as follows. A long-standing feud between Danes and Frisians had apparently been settled by a marriage between Hildeburh, a princess of a tribe closely connected with the Danes, and Finn, who, while himself a Jute, ruled the Frisians from his stronghold Finnsburh, situated just outside Friesland. The Hocingas, to which Hildeburh belonged, may have been ethnically Jutes yet subjects of the Danish king. Thus the alliance could have been the easier to forge because both Finn and Hildeburh were of Jutish origin, though members of different tribes. The fact that the feud which was to be renewed after this attempted reconciliation would be between Jutish warriors on either side, who were compelled to it by the supreme duty of revenge, would add tragic poignancy to the tale. For the obligation to avenge a slain leader, a matter of *comitatus* loyalty, took priority over the loyalty of blood-relationship[3]. When Hildeburh's sons were grown enough to bear arms, her brother Hnæf, leader of the 'Half-Danes' ('Jutes' or 'Danes'), had occasion to visit her and her husband King Finn, accompanied by sixty retainers. These guests, while asleep in the hall of Finnsburh after having been well entertained, were suddenly attacked by Finn's men and Hnæf, as well as his sister's sons, along with many warriors on both sides, was slain. But Hengest, who succeeded Hnæf as leader of the Half-Danes, had by then got himself with his men into some strongly protected position from which they could not have been dislodged except with more loss of Finn's Jutes than he could risk. So Finn accepted a truce, proposed by Hengest, that they have a great ceremonial funeral for the dead of both sides, and then Hengest and his men would, at least for the winter, become Finn's followers. As members of his *comitatus*, Finn promised them

---

[3] The tragic narrative of 'Cynewulf and Cyneheard' under the entry for 755 in the *Anglo-Saxon Chronicle* is a good example in prose of a similar conflict of loyalties.

the same excellent treatment he accorded his own Frisian warriors. Hengest's motive seems to have been revenge, which could be more surely carried out if he gained a respite by this postponement. Hengest is most likely to have suffered a profound mental struggle, torn as he was between the heinousness of accepting service with Finn, whose people had slain his own leader Hnæf, and the basic Germanic duty of exacting vengeance for Hnæf. After spending the winter with Finn, who was probably not responsible for the initial outbreak of the fighting, Hengest, taunted by some of his men, plans vengeance deliberately, so ignoring the new loyalty to Finn which his joining his *comitatus* implied. The fight is renewed by some of Hengest's followers acting as *agents provocateurs*, and Finn and all his men are slain. Hildeburh, also perhaps glad of this vengeance though distraught with the conflicting loyalty to her husband Finn, is taken back to her homeland by the victorious Danes.

This tragic tale, so vividly illustrating conflicting Germanic heroic loyalties, is evidently told in its original lay to an audience entirely familiar with its subject-matter. Only the crises, the highlights and dramatic moments, are touched upon, and this very allusively. Hence the unravelling of the details must remain a puzzle to us today. The original lay of the *Fight at Finnsburh* must have been much older than the *Fragment*: and later parts of it treated in a seemingly more advanced style in the 'Tale of Finn' in *Beowulf*. Yet while the style and tone of the *Fragment* suggest an early date, the occasional irregularities of its metre would point to a later period. The appearance of Hengest in it means that it is the one poem of the ancient Germanic tradition which would have had a specifically Anglo-Saxon interest for the reasons adduced earlier. Both Finn and Hnæf are mentioned in *Widsith* (27, 29), which suggests that their story was well-known on the Germanic Continent as well as in England. Most of the *Fragment* is in dramatic direct speech but lines 34–42 is a piece of heroic narrative showing the earliest expression of the Germanic spirit at its best and most moving.

WALDERE

Two quite separate fragments of verse written in the language of the later tenth century discovered on two leaves in the Royal Library at Copenhagen in 1860 is all that remains of a late copy of an original probably as old as the eighth century, of a romantic heroic poem which must have numbered at least 1000 lines. It is the earliest Anglo-Saxon romantic poem that tells, allusively and dramatically, with the usual assumption that its audience is already familiar with its story, a tale which can only be partially pieced together from later versions, of the flight of the betrothed lovers Waldere or Walther, the Gothic prince of Aquitane, and Hildegyth or Hildegund, a Burgundian princess, from the Court of Attila the Hun, where they had long been hostages. Fleeing with valuable treasure, they are intercepted and attacked by a certain Guthhere, or Gunther, and his followers. Waldere faces overwhelming odds but is victorious single-handed, after some dramatic exchanges between him and Guthhere, to whom he had offered a gift of treasure and peace which had been rejected. According to the earliest other version, *Waltharius*, in tenth-century Latin hexameters, the lovers then journey home to Aquitane, to marriage, and long prosperity.

Waldere is almost entirely in direct dramatic speech. There is Hildegyth's stirring exhortation to her lover to fight well and win in a right cause which God will decide justly, and Waldere's and Guthhere's exchange of challenges in which weapons and armour are particularly extolled. Famous Germanic characters are named – Welund the smith, and Theodoric the Goth, both of whom appear in *Deor*. The heroic personified swords with names of especial power which seem to have been characteristic of heroic poetry occur here with Mimming, Welund's most famous work, given by Theodoric to Widia (Wudga elsewhere in Anglo-Saxon heroic verse), the Gothic hero Vidigiao, and now possessed by Waldere. In Hagena, who had not only been Waldere's companion and friend at Attila's Court, but also Guthhere's vassal, there is the tragic conflict of loyalties in a noble hero which is a prominent motif in the *Finnsburh Fragment* and the 'Tale of Finn' in *Beowulf*. For it seems that Hagena, loyal to his great friend Waldere, is forced by his duty to his lord, Guthhere, to act against Waldere, though he appears to have refused to share in the attack on him. Attila the Hun is referred to again in *Widsith*; and it may be that the Guthhere of this poem is the famous Guthhere the Burgundian in *Widsith*, Gunnar in Old Norse tradition.

Despite the extremely difficult and inevitably disrupted reconstruction of the story of which these are but disjointed fragments, the poem's vivid, intensely moving, dramatic speeches provide an appeal that only serves to accentuate the loss of an epic of which these two extant pieces are both stirring and poetical. From linguistic evidence, the poem must have been in existence by King Alfred's time; its tone and style suggest the *Beowulf* period or a little later. Its Christian references to God in an otherwise

Germanic heroic environment would seem to suggest clerical authorship. Yet it is especially the unexpected romantic appeal of this tale of true love –implicit rather than explicit– that is most memorable. *Waldere* contrasts markedly with *Wulf and Eadwacer*, for it is a tale of exciting adventure in fighting, in which the love interest is merely implied, not expressed. Waldere and Hildegyth are, like the married couples of the Germani as described by Tacitus, comrades in toil and in fight whose relationship is practical.

WIDSITH

The longest and also the oldest of the five poems under consideration here is *Widsith*, which is 143 lines in the **Exeter Book**. First assembled probably in the late seventh century it appears in its extant form in the usual classical Anglo-Saxon of the Benedictine Renaissance period, since its unique copy was made, like those of the rest of the Codex, in one of the leading cultural centres of Wessex. Like the other Anglo-Saxon poems, it owes its title to its editors; here, however, the title is most clearly appropriate. For the poem is a portrayal of the life and work of the ideal *scop* through that of a fictitious one symbolically named *Widsith*, 'far-traveller'. This imaginary *scop* Widsith, while describing his marvellous skill as a poet, provides a sort of catalogue of notable historical and legendary characters and events of that Germanic heroic tradition which the Anglo-Saxons had inherited, and still cherished in their entertainments in their mead-halls. The poet seems to have based his work primarily on three of those mnemonic metrical lists of notables and famous tribes, which had been handed down from remoter times, which still survived or were imitated in Old Icelandic literature as late as the thirteenth century, and which were termed *thulas*. The Latinized list in the *Germania* (chapter 40) may be a relic of one such ancient *thula*.

Widsith consists of a nine-line prologue introducing the *scop* Widsith, a nine-line epilogue of concluding general observations, and the poem proper of 120 lines –one long speech of the *scop* himself which falls clearly into three parts– with a few more lines that seem to have been later interpolations. Each of the three divisions, or *fitts*, of the poem proper may be seen to comprise a *thula* followed by a narrative or comment glorifying the poet in his far-flung journeys and his service to noble rulers, or treating of Germanic history or legend. These ancient lists, formulaic in character, and in an older type of metre than the *scop*'s own material, deal with kings, tribes, and notables from the Germanic fourth to sixth centuries, and follow respectively these more or less set patterns. The first are of the type 'Ætla

21

ruled the Huns, Eormanric the Goths'(18); the second 'I was with the Huns and with the Goths'(57); and the third 'I sought Hethca and Beadeca and the Herelings'(112). There are episodes concerning famous heroes known elsewhere in Anglo-Saxon poetry, such as Eormanric the historical king of the Goths of the later fourth century, Offa the ruler of Angeln and ancestor of Offa the Great of Mercia, and Ingeld of the Heathobards, referred to in *Beowulf* and the subject of a lost lay celebrating his tragic part in a notorious blood-feud. Eormanric and Alboin (here called Ælfwine), the last king of the Lombards, all played a part in the life of this ideal and so long-lived imaginary poet.

The nine-line Prologue is followed by a few introductory lines of a gnomic character leading on to the beginning of the first *thula* at line 18 – a list of rulers commencing with Attila the Hun, a further eighteen lines in length. Then the poet, in his own style, treats of episodes of Offa of Angeln and of the blood-feud which ended the glory of Heorot, Hrothgar's wondrous hall which is the scene of Beowulf's earlier exploits, and refers to the tragedy of Ingeld. Offa is most highly praised, as indeed are all the notable rulers visited by Widsith. But this special glorification of Offa, since he was the ancestor of the great Offa of Mercia of the later eighth century, may indicate that the composition of the poem was completed at a Mercian centre. Some boasting by the imaginary *scop* of the extent of his wanderings, the vastness of the material he has collected for his poetic compositions and the great esteem in which he has been held, leads to the second *thula* at line 57 commencing this time with the slightly varied formula 'I was with . . .'. This extends for thirty lines: and then Widsith returns to the praise of Eormanric with which he had begun (88 ff.) and of the generosity towards him of both the Ostrogothic king and his queen in recognition of his outstanding skill.

The second and third *thulas* are joined by a passage (103–8) in which Widsith describes how he and another *scop*, Scilling, entertained Eormanric's Court to the accompaniment of the harp to win the very highest praise.

After the third *thula* with the formula 'I sought . . .' of a dozen lines (112–124), Widsith ends his speech with more general reflections on his triumph as a singer and a little of that moralizing in which the Anglo-Saxons found pleasure.

The Epilogue, its final nine lines (135–43), rounds off the poem symmetrically in relation to the prologue of identical length. Having introduced the poem with some account of the imaginary *scop* Widsith, the poet ends with an edifying piece of moralizing on the profession of minstrelsy in general.

DEOR

From internal evidence it is evident that *Deor* is of a later date than *Widsith*. Yet, although it is occasionally considered to belong to the elegiac group with which it has some affinities, it would seem more appropriate to treat it here as another of the poems of Germanic tradition with which we are concerned. For, like *Widsith*, it also treats of a fictional *scop* and part of his life-story. At the same time, however, it deals with a number of characters from ancient Germanic history and legend. Again, it shares with the fragmentary *Wulf and Eadwacer*, also in the **Exeter Book**, the use of a lyric refrain – a device unknown in Anglo-Saxon verse apart from these two poems. For this reason, it may not be entirely accidental that *Deor* is immediately followed by *Wulf and Eadwacer* in this anthology of lyric poems. It was once believed that the stanzaic form in Anglo-Saxon was unique to *Deor* until the discovery of an Elizabethan transcript of the poem now known as *The Seasons of Fasting* made from one of the Cotton manuscripts burned in 1731 provided us with an example of a much longer stanzaic piece of verse. It is a versified homily of 230 lines divided into stanzas of eight lines each; but its stanzaic divisions are not specially indicated in the manuscript as are those of *Deor*, nor is its stanzaic structure combined, as in *Deor*, with a terminal refrain.

Each of the groups of unequal length (from three to eight lines) into which *Deor* is divided, is marked off as a stanza in the **Exeter Book** by the use of an initial capital; and, except the sixth (28–35), is concluded with an identical line commonly regarded as a refrain. Lacking this refrain, the sixth group is not distinguished from the seventh in the manuscript, and in it the otherwise regular special sign placed at the end of each group-refrain is absent. The resultant irregularity has led to the belief that the sixth group is a later interpolation, especially since its homiletic tone would appear not to accord with the rest of the poem, and since its presence either makes the poem end with one exceptionally long stanza or otherwise upsets its schematic structure by including a stanzaic group without a refrain. But a homiletic moralizing passage of this type at the end of a set of *exempla* of unfortunate Germanic notables, and preceding the *scop*'s final meditation on his own private misfortune, is not inappropriate in fact in an Anglo-Saxon poem. Nor, to an Anglo-Saxon audience, would its Christian tone seem inconsistent with the traditional matter of the rest of the poem.

An evidently imaginary *scop* symbolically named *Deor* ('noble', 'excellent'), adopting an almost similar literary device to *Widsith*, cites in five successive stanzas examples of famous Germanic characters who suffered great misfortunes which could yet be overcome. Welund the magic smith, Beadohild ravished by Welund in revenge for her father's barbarous cruelty to him, and the unknown woman Mæthhild whose love brought sorrow – are from ancient Germanic legend. And to history belong Theodoric, the Gothic king of the late fifth and early sixth century, and Eormanric, ruler of the Ostrogoths, so much admired by the poet of *Widsith*. An apparent period of exile is implied as Theodoric's misfortune, and the sufferings of Eormanric's subjects under his tyranny explain his presence. The sixth group of lines runs on in the manuscript into the final group in which the *scop* Deor tells of his own misfortune. It is not certain whether, in view of the failure to indicate the sixth group, the whole passage down to the final refrain (35–42) should be taken as forming one long stanza, or whether, as is usual among editors, the two groups should be taken as separate. In the former case the poem will divide into six parts, the five *exempla* of misfortune overcome, and a final homily and personal reflection by its author.

It is inevitable that the very allusiveness of the poet's style is likely to cause difficulty of interpretation to the modern reader unacquainted with the details of the legendary and historical characters dealt with in the poem although the language in itself is very simple. But the audience for which it was intended could be safely assumed by the poet to have been thoroughly familiar with the ancient traditions he used.

The refrain has usually been translated as 'That was overcome; so may this be' but its interpretation, which is important for an understanding of the whole basic philosophy of the poem, is still in doubt. For it is not really clear whether the poet is saying that, just as the five Germanic notables he has cited overcame their misfortunes, so too may others; or, whether it is merely a stoical statement that only time will decide the outcome. With its translation, however, as 'That passed away; so may this!' with the meaning in the earlier stanzas of 'That grief passed; so can this one,' the final stanza acquires a twist; for 'that' refers to Deor's former *prosperity*, now passed away as completely as ancient grief.

This so-called refrain is more a repetitive emphasis of the moral of the poem than a lyric refrain in the technical sense – introduced, it would seem, to reinforce the lesson of the piece rather than for any metrical aesthetic purpose.

There is no definite evidence regarding the date of composition of the poem; for, while its occasional Alfredian forms among the more normal late tenth-century classical Anglo-Saxon of the **Exeter Book** would suggest that it must have existed as early as the eighth century, its apparent affinities with the courtly or *skaldic* poetry of Iceland would preclude one much before the end of the ninth century. On the whole shortly before 900 would seem to be by far the most likely.

The importance of *Deor* is threefold. Historically, its use of ancient Germanic traditional material endorses the belief that the Anglo-Saxon *scop* was well-provided with a fund of legends from which he could freely borrow whenever he needed to. Stylistically, its stanzaic form and unusual refrain accord it a permanent place in the history of the development of English metre (alongside *The Seasons of Fasting* and *Wulf and Eadwacer* as we have already observed). Aesthetically, its blend of lines and stanzas of varying length with an impressive refrain that is also ambiguous in its import, is such as to set the listener thinking.

WULF AND EADWACER

This nineteen-line fragment which immediately follows *Deor* in the **Exeter Book**, derives its title from the names of two of its characters: Wulf, believed by some critics to be an outlaw and the speaker's paramour, and Eadwacer, her detested husband. Others have taken Wulf to be the outlawed husband and Eadwacer the woman's gaoler, who has forced his unwelcome attentions upon her. The 'whelp' (15), according to the first theory, is the husband's child, which Wulf is carrying away to the forest; according to the second, Wulf's. Nothing is known about any of them but all three were clearly protagonists in some remembered old Germanic story[4]. It is for this reason, and because of its use of a refrain reminiscent of *Deor*, that this

---

[4] According to Kemp Malone, 'Two English *Frauenlieder*', *Studies in Old English Literature in Honor of Arthur Brodeur* (University of Oregon, 1963), pp. 106–11, the poem may be a survival of Germanic folksongs once sung by women. It is to be assumed that the identity of the protagonists may ultimately be traced to some such source.

obscure yet intensely moving piece is included here in the group of poems of Germanic tradition.

The lady and Wulf are on separate islands, kept apart by the cruel Eadwacer. Either the lady's own people or even the fierce inhabitants of Wulf's desolate island might have received him: but they can never come together. She sits in tears and misery, comforted by Eadwacer's embraces which are both pleasurable and loathsome to her. It is doubting thoughts of her love, not hunger, that make her miserable. Wulf will carry their wretched offspring to the forest.

Metrically *Wulf and Eadwacer* is a unique curiosity. Its structure, in so far as its incomplete state will allow such consideration, is not really stanzaic, though the use of the refrain may suggest this. On the other hand, the refrain consists of a line and a half, unlike that in *Deor*, which is a normal line, and its occurrence only twice makes it hardly a refrain in the usual sense, though it clearly adds to the lyric effect of the whole. This poem and *The Wife's Lament* are the only real love-poems in Anglo-Saxon – the gnomic verses in the **Exeter Book** on the return of the sailor to his Frisian wife and *The Husband's Message* being insufficiently so to merit inclusion within this category. But, of the two, *Wulf and Eadwacer* comes much nearer to that kind of romantic love-lyric which began to flower in England under direct Continental influence from the twelfth century onward. In this respect also, it is unique, for the egocentric expression of love did not normally find a place in ancient Germanic culture. This love-poem is certainly, as it seems, popular in origin, rather than courtly. Its simple, almost naked expression of passion lacks any of the sophistication of the poetry of 'courtly love'. The fact that it is placed in the mouth of a woman, too, would support the view that it sprang rather from popular than from courtly culture. Its date of composition, as with so many Anglo-Saxon poems, cannot be determined more than roughly. Its Anglian origin is suggested by the language, and that there was a copy of it in existence as early as around 900 is indicated by some Alfredian forms.

In fine, the poem's appeal seems to lie in its obscurity – its thematic patterning, its style: in the refrain, in the pathetic fallacy of rainy weather and weeping; in the shifts of syntax and line lengths; in its unmetrical and plaintive *Wulf min Wulf* (13). Allusive and incomplete as the poem is, it is one of the most passionate of love lyrics that has survived in Anglo-Saxon.

(B) FOLK TRADITION

GNOMIC VERSE

There are extant two heterogeneous collections of Gnomic Verse called Maxims, in addition to occasional examples to be found in other poems, such as those which link the two main parts of *The Wanderer*[5] or occur as moralizing comments in *Beowulf*.[6] One of these, the Exeter Gnomes or Maxims *(Maxims I)*, extends to 204 lines in the **Exeter Book**, while the other, the Cotton Maxims *(Maxims II)*, only 66 lines long, is in a Cottonian manuscript of the *Anglo-Saxon Chronicle* from the eleventh century.

The gnome, maxim, proverb, or brief, pithy, sententious saying was employed in Anglo-Saxon verse sometimes to expound proverbial or folk wisdom, sometimes more elaborately to affirm a moral, or define a virtue or vice. Their concise brevity, their invariable appositeness, framed in the alliterative pattern of Anglo-Saxon verse, endows them with a trenchant memorability that is the outstanding quality of the type. To the Anglo-Saxon poet (of whose literary and folk heritage they formed a part), the more characteristic gnomes provided a fund of moral aphorisms upon which he was able to draw whenever a particular episode in a poem needed to be enlightened, or its significance enforced, by the sententious assertion of a widely accepted truth. Both the Exeter and Cotton collections of gnomes seem to have been familiar to an Anglo-Saxon audience and presenting a wide variety of subject matter and spirit. In fact they lack a central unity, thus making it possible to detect where discordant gnomes have been grafted into the alliterative pattern. The gnomes that comprise these collections vary in length from brief half-lines to more extended passages of ten to twelve lines; and, they also vary in spirit and substance. Some are older than others and bear no traces of Christian influence, obviously surviving from a primitive culture. Others are of later origin, more sophisticated in spirit, and either rooted in the Christian tradition or definitely modified or moulded by it.

The interest of these gnomic verses is mainly in the light they may throw on native folklore and traditional patterns of thinking, though, like most Anglo-Saxon verse, they inextricably blend elements of ancient pre-

---

[5] Lines 64–72.

[6] B C Williams, *Gnomic Poetry in Anglo-Saxon*, p. 29, classifies 23 passages varying in length from one half-line to five lines in length as unmistakably gnomic in spirit.

Christian tradition with Christian piety. Typical are the opening lines of *Maxims II* which consist of a series of gnomes or maxims followed from line 54 by a kind of pious Christian epilogue which shows something of the elegiac quality.

Maxims I occur in three sections, or fitts, in the manuscript. But they show no marked poetic quality. However, in them there are perhaps more of the gnomic traces of ancient oral tradition. With the statement that 'Sagacious men shall swap speech'(4), the compiler begins a catalogue of whatever he remembered of the heterogeneous gnomic and sententious material at his disposal. So, the building of a ship suggests to him the famous lines on the return of the sailor to his Frisian wife (second fitt, 24–9), noticed earlier as one of the very rare approaches to love-poetry in Anglo-Saxon. *Maxims II*, in the same hand as the *Menologium* and the *Anglo-Saxon Chronicle*, seem to have been regarded along with the poetic Church calendar as a kind of preamble to the *Chronicle*; and, with their religious epilogue, show a slight sense of form, whereas *Maxims I* are a mere string of disconnected gnomic statements.

Some of the obviously older gnomes relate to the physical world and compress into a few words primitive knowledge of nature, realistic observation of the characteristics of animals, and details of weather. It is clear that, in some instances, gnomes of earlier origin have been subsequently amended to make them harmonize with the Christian mood and tradition. Such is the passage of seven lines with which the second fitt of Maxims I begins: 'Frost shall freeze . . .'.

A passage from *Maxims II* (5–9) reveals the same remoulding of old gnomes under a Christian influence. And, once again, the dovetailing of old and new is evident in the joining: '*Wyrd* is cruellest . . .'.

Some of the gnomes in these two collections are clearly related to the ancient folkways of primitive Germanic life, briefly but sharply reflecting the Heroic Age in spirit and custom. Such are the four lines (65–9) which conclude the third fitt of *Maxims I* ('The shield shall be ready . . .'). The heroic spirit is unmistakable, the reflection of the *comitatus* as sharp, as in any passage of battle poem or pagan epic.

Another passage in *Maxims I* (second fitt, 11–22) bears the mark of derivation from old Germanic custom and rite. It constitutes a unit describing the qualities requisite for worthy rule by king and queen. The passage begins with an allusion to the custom of marriage by purchase, and reference is made to the virtues of warlike valour and generosity in a king; but thereafter the passage is developed wholly as a portrait of the ideal queen. The high position of woman in Germanic society is indicated throughout, and the reference to the function of the queen as cup-bearer suggests the Germanic ritual in accordance with which at the banquet in *Beowulf* it is the queen, Wealtheow, who offers the hall-cup first to Hrothgar and then to each of his guests in turn[7].

A particularly interesting insertion in *Maxims I* is the famous 'Frisian woman' passage, which follows close on the passage just cited. The opening lines (24–9) are obviously lyric in spirit rather than gnomic. Line 30 marks a resumption of the gnomic mood, and succeeding lines reveal characteristic devices of gnomic form. The passage seems to offer one more illustration in these collections of the welding of materials varying in age and subject matter.

Both sets of *Maxims* must have been compiled by ecclesiastics, in view of the Christian and sometimes learned piety which they display beside the traditional lore. No dates can be assigned to them, since much of the matter is clearly inherited from the earliest Anglo-Saxon times and some of it is pre-Christian, while some of the sententious moralizing evidently belongs to the period of the Anglo-Saxon homilies of the tenth century. The compilations of such mixed material as is found in the extant texts give the impression of their being incomplete and more or less casual collections of *memorabilia* assembled for purposes of edification, both secular and religious. Though there may not now appear to be much aesthetic appeal in these writings, it must be remembered that the Anglo-Saxons found genuine entertainment as well as edification in listening to moral aphorisms and *sententiae*, as is shown by their sporadic inclusion even in *Beowulf.*

CHARMS

Of considerable note among the Germanic cultural inheritances of the Anglo-Saxons was the use of Charms or magic incantations as remedies against natural disorders, diseases, or hostile witchcraft, or as general protectives. The adaptation of pagan religious practices to Christian purposes (on the advice of St Gregory the Great to St Augustine of Canterbury) would account for the preservation in medical –especially herbal– recipes in religious houses, in tenth and eleventh century

---

[7] Lines 612b–18a.

manuscripts, of some twelve metrical charms intercalated among prose ceremonial directions and related matter. The poetic quality of these charms is not of the first order – their irregular metres indicating oral traditions older than those of classical Anglo-Saxon poetry. Their interest, however, especially to cultural anthropologists, lies in their curious mixture of pagan traditional magic and Christian ritual. To the layman, it is their unexpected freshness and vitality that appeal. It is not always easy to distinguish between these verse-incantations and their prose accompaniment, but twelve charms are generally recognized.

The fullest of these charms, 'For Unfruitful Land', is unique as a specimen of Anglo-Saxon agricultural rites. Though the use of texts from the Old and New Testament, masses, holy names and objects, is Christian, the old heathen practices and formulas that form its basis are recognizable throughout. Thus, several of the new Christian religious substitutions seem to have been chosen because they hardly differed in spirit from the magical atmosphere of their pagan originals, an example of which is the use of the sign of the cross. Itself a religious Christian element in its application, it assumes a magical significance when the crosses are to be made of 'quickbeam' (aspen wood), a special kind of wood intended to quicken, enliven, and encourage the growth of a piece of land; when their arms are to be inscribed with the names of the four evangelists (a usage alien to ecclesiastical ritual); and when they are to be laid at the four sides of the land.

Nor are the pagan elements purely magic. The first two verse passages, in fact, are Christianized hymns to the sun god and Mother Earth – relics of an older religion. And, the two other verse parts of the text are also not charms. All four invoke the help of either a deified being or of God and His saints, whereas authentic charms evince the personal power of the protagonist and generally assume the form of commands rather than supplications. Admittedly, several of the elements are magical in origin and atmosphere but the ritual itself is a religious one. That the introductory paragraph should refer to the use of the charm 'if any harm has been done to them by sorcery or witchcraft' seems to imply the operation of magical forces; but the distinction between religion and magic is often blurred in theory and almost non-existent in practice. To the simple Anglo-Saxon mind the use of charms was a harmless practice providing witchcraft, sorcery, or 'black magic' were not involved, which were definitely anti-social. They were permissible, however, when applied against a hostile tribe. There are two parts to the text. The first concerns ceremonies in honour of the sun and relate to the grassland; the second, ceremonies in honour of Mother Earth, who is invoked to bless and fructify the arable land.

Preparations are to be made while it is still dark. 'Take then at night, ere dawn, four sods from the four sides of the land and mark how they stood before.' The four sides represent the entire area, the marking of the sods the need to reproduce every detail exactly; for, on the latter, and a strict conformity to tradition, depended success in ritual.

Oil, honey, yeast, milk of all the cattle that feed on the land, parts of every kind of tree (except hard trees) that grow on the land, and parts of every sort of herb (except burdock), are then taken. Holy water is added and allowed to drip three times through the objects on to the bottom of the sods while an entirely Christian formula is pronounced: a verse from Genesis, the invocation of the Trinity, and the Paternoster. The Paternoster is said as often as the other, that is, three times. Dew was probably used in the original charm – the holy water representing a Christianization of this part. As completeness is a feature of magic, the exception of hard trees and burdock is somewhat difficult to explain.

Next the sods are carried into the church where a priest is required to sing four masses over them, while their green sides are turned towards the altar. The number of masses is identical with the number of sods but their turning towards the altar would point to an earlier ceremony during which the rays of the rising sun actually fell on them, and only on to them, through an aperture, so that its power was thus concentrated and not weakened. From the text it is to be understood that the midday sun was included as the sods are to 'be brought ere sunset to where they stood before'.

The inscription of the names of the four evangelists on the arms of the crosses and their utterance over the pits made by cutting away the sods is another Christianization. The crosses are laid in the pits and the sods placed over them. With the ninefold repetition of the *Crescite* formula, the power of the sun is transferred to the land. There is nothing remarkable about the introduction of the four evangelists since the number 'four' occurs repeatedly in the charm with the sides of the land, quarters of the heavens, sods, masses, and crosses. What is puzzling, however, is the reason for the inscription of the names on the crosses and the burial of the latter in the pits. That stones are inscribed or even buried is not strange but that crosses should, as is the case here, certainly is. However, it is not unknown for a cross to follow a corpse into the graveyard to be buried later as a symbol of the victory of the soul over the body and was probably a survival of an earlier heathen custom. Here the crosses represent the fructifying power of the sun and of the four cardinal points from which blow rain-bearing winds.

The adoration of the sun and a prayer to the sun god to fructify the land follow next. The priest (or magician) turns towards the east, bows down to the earth nine times and utters a prayer that at some time in the past must have been a pagan invocation but is now so heavily disguised by Christian additions that it is hard to tell which is which (except for the direct reference to 'the truly holy Mary'). At the conclusion of the hymn the celebrant turns three times with the course of the sun (thus showing his acceptance of its mastery over him and soliciting its favour) before prostrating himself on the earth so as to transmit his own fertility to it.

With the addition of Christian prayers, such as the litany, the original magical import of this humbling before a pagan divinity was lost. The litany is followed by the *Tersanctus, Benedicite, Magnificat* and Paternoster.[8] These four liturgical prayers were carefully selected to assure good crops (which, after all, was the purpose of the charm): the *Tersanctus* because it includes the *pleni sunt coeli et 'terra' gloria tua* (heaven and 'earth' are full of thy glory); the *Benedicite* because it calls upon *universa germinantia in terra* (all things which sprout forth on the earth) to bless the Lord; the *Magnificat* because of its *esurientes implevit bonis* (He has filled the hungry with good things); and the Paternoster because of its petition *panem nostrum quotidianum da nobis hodie* (give us this day our daily bread). All these prayers both praise the Lord for His munificence and solicit His aid in adding to His glory by an increase of crops on the land. The outstretched arms of the celebrant produce a likeness to the sacred Rood which, together with Christ and holy Mary are commended to be praised in the hope that it

---

[8] The *Tersanctus* ('thrice *Sanctus*' or 'Holy, holy, holy'), the *Benedicite* ('Praise . . .'), the *Magnificat* ('It magnifies . . .'), and the Paternoster ('Our Father . . .' or 'The Lord's Prayer') are Roman Catholic liturgical prayers. The first is uttered jointly by clergy and laity before the *Prefatio* ('Preface') of the Mass. The *Benedicite* occurs in Daniel 3.76, in the Latin Vulgate but not in the Authorised Version and is the hymn of praise sung by Shadrach, Mesach and Abad-nego on their being cast into the fiery furnace by order of Nebuchadnezzar. The *Magnificat* (Luke 1.46–55) is the hymn sung by the Virgin Mary in answer to the greetings of her cousin Elizabeth.

may be of benefit to the owner of the land 'and of all those subject to him'. This concludes the first part of the charm relating to grassland.

The second part of the charm is concerned with arable land and it is Mother Earth, instead of the sun god, who is addressed. But there is no conflict of interests and the transition is smoothly effected with the words: 'When all this is done . . .'. The taking of unknown seed from beggars is intended as an offering to Mother Earth and its value enhanced by its mysterious magical flavour. Implicit is the understanding that the reward will be twice as large as the sacrifice. All the ploughing implements are then collected. A hole is bored in the ploughtail into which are put incense, fennel, hallowed salt (all usually part of ritual sacrifice) and hallowed soap. This last ingredient occurs nowhere else and the reason for its use is obscure. The unknown seed is placed on the plough and then the hymn to Mother Earth is sung. The thrice-repeated word *Erce* of the first half of the first line is a complete mystery and may, it is assumed, have some connection with Ceres, the mother of Proserpine, the goddess of agriculture. The 'mother of earth' of the second half of the same line is equally mysterious and the entire line may have meant nothing to the celebrant who chanted it. The invocation to Erce is intended as a protection against the evil influences of black magic, the Christian elements of which can be removed without damage to the remaining part. The second half of the invocation is an intercession that the produce may not be spoilt by any foe, that it may be secure from any harm done to it by sorcery, 'that no witch so eloquent, nor man so potent, | there be to pervert the words thus pronounced (28–9).

The plough is then 'driven forth and the first furrow cut' during which Earth, the mother of men, is invoked to fill the land with 'food for the benefit of men'. A small loaf kneaded with milk and holy water and baked is laid in the furrow as an additional offering to Mother Earth as a reminder of what is expected of her and what she can expect to receive when she yields good crops. The ceremony is then concluded with a repetition of the threefold recitation of the *Crescite* and the Paternoster that occurred at the beginning.

The Christian reviser of the charm was evidently lacking in poetic skill for he is monotonously repetitive throughout.

In 'The Nine Herbs Charm', the magical effect of the herbs is intensified by an account of their achievements in times past.

A stanza is devoted to each herb of which Mugwort may be taken to be fairly representative. It begins with an allusion to an outstanding feat, followed by a declaration that it is mightier than 'three', mightier than 'thirty' (numbers that represent a magical group, a strong band of enemies). As such it can help against poison, infection, and 'the foe that fares through the land' in search of victims. Regenmeld has been explained as a woman's name, a placename, and a solemn announcement. Mugwort is known to have distinguished itself there and is certain to repeat that performance in the present circumstances. The explicit nature of the circumstances referred to, however, is obscure.

From the internal evidence of the charm, there are nine parallel passages of which the first three have come down to us intact. Each one ends with the assertion that the herb it refers to avails against 'the foe who fares through the land' and is 'power against poison, power against infection'. The parallel wording of these cannot have been accidental. So, Mugwort distinguished itself at Regenmeld; Plantain was overrun and trodden upon by chariots, queens, brides and bulls, but it resisted them; *Stune* had withstood a serpent's venom and expelled its evil influence; Camomile had distinguished itself at Alorford, thus restoring the complete parallel with mugwort, but the reference to 'the foe who fares through the land' is lacking; *Wergulu* was specially selected to cross the sea at the command of a seal, and here the parallel with mugwort is restored in the declaration that it is meant 'to heal the harm of other venoms'.

The treatment of the last three herbs is different: the Apple, which from the prose passage at the end of the charm seems to be original, is described in two lines while the others are lost entirely. Two imported plants, Chevril and Fennel, replace these. The Christian reviser responsible for this part must have realized the value of the story about each herb and decided to invent the legend that they were specially created by the Lord as He hung on the cross, so that, here too, the parallel is maintained, although the atmosphere is different. Their power is derivative not inherent, as they had been created by Christ at the very moment at which, by His death, He had earned God's favour and grace for all men rich and poor, happy and miserable alike.

To crown their own achievements, Woden himself comes to their aid against the Evil One, with his nine glory-twigs (each of which represents the initial letter of the nine herbs in runes) which he uses to smite the adder. Thanks to their power, it splits into nine pieces.

Their worth undeniably proved thus, the power of the nine herbs is used to counteract various kinds of poison which are enumerated and described as to their colour, appearance, symptoms, and the direction from which they are likely to attack the victim. Implicit in the reference to Woden is the suggestion that, like the god, the victim can proceed to the attack against any poison now that he knows enough about all of them. The Christian reviser, of course, improved on the idea by inserting the line about Christ.

Having recounted the various powers of the herbs, both individually and together, the magician declares that his power is equally great for he alone knows running water of which snakes are afraid. He blows away the poison and to prevent its return he must find an appropriate place to which to banish it. The roots of weeds that it cannot harm, the immensity of the seas, all salty water which dissolve it – these are his answer. With this description of the final disposal of the poison the charm ends.

There is little difficulty with the prose passage. *Lombescyrse* (lamb's-cress) and *netele* (nettle) respectively replace *stune* and *wergulu* in the list of plants, whereas there is no change in the order and names of the other plants to be found in the poetic formula. A few directions are given for the preparation of the herbs and the singing of the charm. Infections, *onflygan*, were generally supposed to enter through the ears and mouth, so that the remedy against them was also sung into the mouth and the ears of the patient; in the case of a wound caused by the bite of a snake the charm was to be sung on the wound, of course.

There is little certainty as to the disease meant by the title, 'Against a Dwarf', but from the internal evidence of the charm, 'his limbs began to cool' (4), it probably indicates a fever.

The interpretation of the charm hinges on what is meant by *spiderwiht* (1). The spider is a benevolent spirit that has come in to help drive out the disease spirit, for which purpose it uses its web to bridle the dwarf (1–2a). The disease spirit is told that it is going to be used as the spider's steed, and that it will be harnessed. So it will have to obey the spider (2b–3a). Both set off from the land and 'his limbs began to cool' so that the fever began to leave off (3b–4). At the same time the dwarf's sister (another spider) came in and she completed the cure and declared on oath that neither the patient nor anyone else would be troubled with this particular disease if it was known how to obtain and recite the charm (5–9).

35

The charm is to be sung three times, first into the left ear, then into the right one, then over the sick man's head. As right and left are both mentioned, they seem to have no particular magical significance, and the fact of its being done seems accidental.

Next a virgin must go to him and hang it around his neck. Since the charm refers to two spiders and seven wafers with the names of the Seven Sleepers[9] written on them, presumably they are bound up in a pouch or bag which is then hung around the patient's neck.

The general purpose and meaning of the charm 'For a Sudden Stitch' are clear. It is a cure for stinging pain, suddenly felt by the victim and supposedly caused by 'mighty women', hags, elves, and gods. That diseases may be caused by the attacks of evil spirits is a primitive belief common the world over. From the wording of the charm (18–20) it is to be inferred that rheumatic pains affecting various parts of the body are meant.

Metrically the charm consists of two parts. The first (1–17) is made up of loosely alliterative, irregular lines, possibly divided into four or five stanzas; while the second (18–24) is made up of fairly regular long lines. The most likely explanation is that two different charms got mixed, due to the identical expressions *Hægtessan geweorc* (17) and *hægtessan gescot* (22).

Of importance to the metrical structure, for the meaning of the charm more than for its external form, is a kind of refrain: *Ut lytel spere, gif her inne sy* (4, 10, 13), and *Ut spere næs in spere* (15).

As the first thing the magician needs to be sure of is the cause of the pain, he begins by telling the patient and the spirits that he knows all about it. He heard them when they rode through the air, when they cried out loud (1), when they rode fiercely over the land (2). Their fierceness is stressed by their association with a burial-mound – black magic often being practised in graveyards for the evil power that was to be gained by contact with the dead. The magician warns the patient to shield himself if he is to survive their malice (3). He is not afraid of them and exploits the power he has acquired from his hearing them by pronouncing the exorcismal formula: 'Out little spear, if herein thou be!'(4). He goes on to state that he has not only heard

---

[9] According to early Christian legend, the seven noble youths of Ephesus who fell asleep in a cave while fleeing from the Decian persecution and woke 187 years later.

them but has also seen them. Under cover of a linden shield he witnessed how the mighty women betrayed their own power as they 'sent their screaming spears forth'(5–7). They are now deprived of their power because someone has seen them. Their secret is out and a defence has been found (8–9).

He need not use stealth. On the contrary, he will face them and send an arrow back! This he can do, because he knows his adversaries. He is not afraid of 'mighty women' and their darts, and confidently repeats the formula: 'Out little spear, if herein thou be!'(10). He is well-armed and his own weapons have preternatural powers. A smith has forged a knife for him, and six smiths have wrought war-spears for him (11–14). At this point one or more lines are missing. The name of the smith is not given, but it is not difficult to guess that it is Welund who is meant – the only smith in Germanic mythology gifted with preternatural powers. The six smiths are a mystery. The *Vǫlundrkviða* mentions three, Vǫlundr, Slagfiðr and Egil. The number six may have been caused by the alliteration *Syx smiðas sætan* (14).

There must have been some connexion between the knife mentioned in line 11 and the knife actually used at the end of the charm. From evidence available, the Anglo-Saxon medical man seems to have always had a knife with him, *læceseax*, which was used for magical purposes.

The help of the smiths and the knife and spears could not fail to be effective; so, with increasing stress, the magician pronounces the exorcismal formula (10, 15–17).

From line 18 onwards the rhythm and the structure of the charm change and there is a fairly straightforward formula. Whether the victim is hit in the skin, the flesh, the blood, or in a limb, his life will no more be endangered, even though he were shot at by a god, an elf or a hag; for, against all of them, the magician knows a defence and he will come to the rescue. Whereas, so far, only 'mighty women' (6) or 'hags' (17), have been mentioned, the charm now speaks of hags, elves and *Æsir*.

Once again the rhythm changes abruptly. The meaning of the final lines, and of the charm as a whole, may become clearer from a comparison with similar charms and magical practices in other countries. Thus, it is believed that a disease may be transferred from a patient to a spear or an arrow, which is then thrown or shot away, if possible into an uninhabited spot where no one can be harmed by it. It could also mean that the various parts of the body - skin, flesh, blood and limb - are touched by a specially prepared spear or knife, which is thrown away afterwards. The knife may have served to apply the salve on the wound or the painful region. At the same time slight incisions may have been made to draw blood and to get at the spirit that had taken possession of the patient. If conditions were made sufficiently unpleasant for it, it would rather leave.

By the 'liquid' at the end of the charm is meant the mixture of butter and herbs of the opening lines of prose. The magical properties of red nettle are strengthened because it must be a plant 'that grows through a house'.

The two charms 'For Loss of Cattle' and the one 'For Theft of Cattle', have so much in common that they are best considered together. Except for the wording of the third one, they can be all regarded as different versions of the same charm. Largely Christianized, their pagan elements are, nevertheless, easy to recognize. The incantatory formula of the last one entitles it to be treated first, but all the others contain elements that are known and practised all over the world and that, therefore, belong to the oldest practices in existence.

The two charms with the one title are slightly different versions of the same charm. Both open with a comparison: this particular theft will be as widely known as is the town of Bethlehem because of the birth of Christ. After this general statement the magician embarks on his spell concerning the stolen cattle or goods. Although ostensibly Christian, their instructions to the magician to turn east, west, south and north, and to say a prayer three times in each direction, are clearly indicative of earlier heathen practices. The magician turns to the four heavens not only because he does not know in which direction the thief has fled, but because, by doing so, he is paying homage to the sun, who is bound to know where the thief is hiding and, so, can enlighten him.

As the method employed in the third charm is similar to the other two, it is reasonable to assume that it contains relics of the incantatory formulas that accompany the magical actions found there. In this one, however, the magical actions are entirely lacking and all that remains is the oral formula.

The Christianization of this charm is confined to the prose opening and to the first line of verse. In addition to the reference to St Helena and her discovery of the True Cross, there is the reminder of Herod's failure to seize Christ: even as Herod was unable to seize Christ, so will the thief be unable to seize any of the owner's goods. It will be impossible to seize or carry away any man's possessions, if he uses this charm; and, if a thief has succeeded so far, he will not keep his booty long, for he will not be able to find a place to hide it till the danger is past. Christ hanging on the cross is reminiscent of the action of stretching oneself on the earth in the form of a cross. The original significance of the action is forgotten and all that survives is the cross, and Christ with whom it is naturally associated.

After the charm is sung, the owner is convinced that he will find his cattle. They will not be driven away too far; he will know where they are and they will not get lost; he will treat them well, and they will not be led away. The promise to treat his cattle well is an admonition to the animals to try and return of their own accord. In magic, every resource is exploited and nothing is too insignificant, for the most trivial detail may have unsuspected magical power.

Next Garmund, a 'servant of God' of whom nothing is known, is invoked to find the cattle, keep and hold them and finally send them home again. He must see to it that the thief 'may never have land to lead them to, nor ground to carry them to, nor houses to hold them in.' If, however, the thief succeeds in carrying them off, he will not escape discovery and punishment: within three days everything about him will be known.

The internal evidence of the charm 'For Delayed Birth', indicates a combination of four or five different practices intended to be performed at different times.

That this charm was said after a miscarriage or an early death had actually occurred is to be understood by the statement that the woman 'must take part of the grave of her own child, wrap it up in black wool and sell it to merchants.'

An analysis of the entire charm presents the following picture. The woman who cannot bring her child to maturity must go to a dead man's grave, step three times over it, and say that she does so to ward off various misfortunes that may occur at the birth of her child. The birth must be propitious – neither slow, nor difficult, nor painful, nor gloomy, nor must it have the evil outcome of a lame child (1–3). Her stepping over the grave signifies victory, that she is stronger than death, even as a warrior steps over the body of his slain opponent to signal his success, for the grave is symbolic of death. This comparison is often expressed in words, but a comparison in actions is no less frequent and more impressive.

So far, the actions are precautions for a happy delivery. After conception, 'when that woman is with child', she repeats the act of stepping over someone. This time, however, it is a live person, her husband. The text states only that she says so (4), but there can be no doubt that she puts her words into practice, or did so originally. The similarity of her actions ought to remind any death-spirit of her power and restrain it from harassing her and killing her child: she steps over her husband with a live child, not with a dying one, with one that will be fully formed and brought forth at the proper time, not with a fated one. In this way she makes sure not to miscarry.

The Christian interpolation occurs here. After some months, when she feels that the child is alive in her womb, she must go to church, and when she is in front of the altar, she must express her thanks to Christ that by His help she is again with child. From the successive stages by which the whole performance unwinds, it is certain that the Christian elements, the going up to the altar and thanking Christ, have replaced an earlier pagan practice. It is hard to tell what the original directions were, but there is no reason to suppose that they prescribed much more than going to a sacred spot and thanking a god, for all the directions and formulas of this charm are short and straightforward.

When she is absolutely certain, after the rites described, that she is going to bear another child, she will put away the sorrow and misery she feels about the death of her former child. She goes to the place where it is buried, takes some earth from the grave, wraps it up in black wool and sells it to merchants with the instruction to re-sell it (8). Her sorrow is represented by the earth of the grave and by the piece of black wool. There is a harking back here to the gloomy birth of an ill child or a dead one. Her grief is embodied in an object that is handed over to someone who will see to its complete disappearance. For merchants wander about the country, going from one place to the other; so, there is no possibility whatever that she will know where her grief has gone to. Nor will she be able to recall it, either literally or figuratively. Neither will any spirit be able to find its way back to trouble her again. Her grief is gone because she has another child to rejoice in.

When the time comes for the birth of the child, and with it the problem as to whether she will have sufficient milk to nourish it, she must take a handful of milk from a cow of one colour, sip it up into her mouth, go to running water and spit it into the stream. Cows of one colour were probably rare in Anglo-Saxon England, so their infrequency, and the difficulty of finding one, gave this kind of milk a rarity to be reckoned with as a magical factor. The charm does not specify the hand from which the milk is sipped up. All that it states is that 'with the same hand she must take a mouthful of water and swallow it'. Running water has a purifying effect which operates on impure evil spirits, so that they are expelled and must find another dwelling. Every precaution is taken to ensure that the spirit will not return to the woman from whom it has gone out; and, when she returns home, she goes another way. She also keeps silent so as to retain the magical force she has absorbed by her actions, by her contact with milk of one colour and with running water. To avoid contact with wandering spirits, she must not look round, for such an action would destroy her magical concentration and allow a spirit to harm the child. To lead them all astray she enters a house other than the one she left.

During these final actions the woman's fasting intensifies the magical effect of her taking the specified milk into her mouth and sipping up running water. For that reason her lactation will be plentiful and nourishing. The Anglo-Saxon mother is convinced that when she can properly feed her child, it will grow up healthy and strong.

The set of magical actions is finished and the magical atmosphere finally broken when she partakes of food in the house of a neighbour.

In the charm 'For the Water-elf Disease', a man possessed by a 'water-elf' may be known by the pale, colourless appearance of his fingernails, his watery, tearful eyes, and the fact that he usually looks down – thus a general listlessness of body and mind. The remedy prescribed is a concoction made up of nineteen herbs, soaked in beer and holy water. The holy water is the only Christian addition in driving away the devils and evil spirits. [There are altogether fifty-two different plants recorded in Anglo-Saxon which occur in the various drinks and salves against elves and devils, whose magical virtues are not very apparent, although they do not seem to have been chosen arbitrarily].

The verse of the incantation is quite irregular, the composer appearing to have only aimed at some syllables beginning with the same consonants, although the irregularity may be due in part to the bad state in which the text has been transmitted to us.

The exact meaning of *wæterælfadl* is not clear. A possible explanation is that 'water-elf disease' is another name for chicken-pox (Dutch *waterpokken*, German *Wasserpocken*). The symptoms might serve to distinguish them from other pocks. The way in which the spots appear and disappear may well have given rise to the belief that they were the tricks of a mischievous elf. Its symptoms are a burning sensation in the affected areas, and when the sores burst a liquid runs out and infects other parts of the body (3–4). Pock or pocks is related to other words denoting goblins, imps, demons (Anglo-Saxon *pucel*, Icelandic *puki*, Shakespeare 'Puck') and the liquid suggests a 'water' elf. As chicken-pox occurs all over the body there is the direction: 'Sing this many times' (beginning of the prose passage).

The main formula (1–5) presents many difficulties, and only line 2 is comparatively clear. So, the magician is seen to have bound up the wounds (1) in order to prevent them from burning or bursting (2); from going further, from spreading and jumping about, that is, disappearing in one place and reappearing in another (3); and from increasing or deepening (4). He himself will hold out for him, will protect him with healing water (5); and with earth, so that the pain abates and ceases (6).

After the first incantation against the working of the elf in general, a second, specially invoking the power of earth, is pronounced many times, on each separate wound to weaken and destroy them altogether. This second incantation is a typically magical device against a water-elf: 'May the earth destroy thee with all her might and main'. It is, of course, natural in magic that earth should be applied and invoked against a water-elf.

The charm 'For a Swarm of Bees' is one of the finest extant Anglo-Saxon charms. Although brief, it succeeds in presenting an attractive picture of the simplicity and faith of the Germanic people. And, despite the problems of its interpretation and form of details, it is simple and straightforward compared with most other charms. Its completeness is striking. In artistic beauty of structure and treatment, it surpasses every other Germanic charm of contemporary or later date. Fully pagan, it is the only pagan bee charm in Germanic countries.

It consists of two verse passages, both preceded by a few words in prose. The verse is the normal alliterative form of Anglo-Saxon poetry, with the stave on the first stress in the second half-line and one or two alliterating words in the first half-line. However, it does not attain the finished form of other Anglo-Saxon poems as the attempt to scan its lines is bound to reveal.

The title explains the meaning and purpose of the charm which is to make a swarm of bees come down in the neighbourhood of the bee-keeper. To prevent their swarming is wrong, since the action is a good thing in itself and is necessary for the increase in the number of hives and the production of honey. Honey, of course, was of great importance to the Anglo-Saxons, since it was the only sweetening stuff they possessed, was the principal ingredient of mead, and was also noted for its medicinal properties.

The charmer takes some earth in his right hand, throws it up into the air and places his right foot on it when it comes down. The action of throwing up the earth with his right hand and catching it under his right foot is not an ordinary one, but is entirely magical, and is intensified by the words that accompany it.

In the first part of the charm the magician states his knowledge of the magic that is in earth and shows that he himself has control of that power by the action he performs and the words he utters. In the second half of the charm he applies his power when the moment of swarming comes. Although the charm forms a unity, some time may actually elapse between its parts. What is important is that the charmer feels the connection and mentally combines the parts. As the swarming of bees is noticeable beforehand by a buzzing sound in the hive, he knows when it is time to make ready and the interval need not be long. Again he starts by performing an action, which is subsequently strengthened by the second charm-formula. At the moment that the queen rises into the air with her followers, he casts gravel or sand over them, thus surrounding them with a magic ring or wall that they are powerless to cross. They are forced to stay within the circle of sand and to come down in the neighbourhood. This time sand is used instead of a clod of earth because sand separates into a great many small grains, so that each bee is caught, as it were, in a separate circle. At the same time the height to which the earth is thrown indicates the height beyond which the bees cannot rise from the ground, and this action serves a double purpose: the bees cannot fly away too far, nor can they settle too high on a tree, where they may be impossible to reach. For the rest, sand is as much part of the earth as clay or any other kind of soil.

The accompanying words complete and explain the magical enchantment. What is not clear, however, is why the bees are addressed as *sigewif*, 'victorious women'.

The aura of magic of 'A Journey Charm' is restricted to the beginning (1–9); otherwise the Christianization is complete. As an example of a magical charm it is a very poor representative of the genre but it possesses a fairly well-developed charm formula which is original though of late provenance, typical of the change that has come over magic. The intense, emotional

43

atmosphere of magic of the earlier charms has been replaced by the intense, emotional atmosphere of popular religion and the forces evoked by the performance of actions and the utterance of words associated with magic are now subject to the intervention of God, the Creator of heaven and earth. There is a request for help, without the compulsion to produce a result, addressed to a selection of great figures in both the Old and the New Testament. And, if the user of this charm is assured of its success, it is not because he dominates the alien forces against which he contends but because the force to which he addresses himself has invited him to pray.

The form of the charm is looser than the others encountered so far. Its metrical weakness is only partly due to the inability of the reviser to attain the right form, but the verse-form itself is changing. There is still a great deal of alliteration, but we also find the beginning of rhyme, if only inside a line (20–21).

The charm is sung against various dangers that may befall a traveller: the stitch of small insects and the bite of snakes, both the instruments of evil spirits (2). It is effective against horrible apparitions (3), and is good 'against the great terror that is loathsome to everyone and against all evil that enters the land' (4–5). The defence against these dangers is the rod or staff by which the charmer protects himself (1) and the charm he sings. The charmer encircles himself with a staff, that is, inscribes in the sand a line by which he is enclosed, for the line is a magical wall that neither insect, nor snake nor evil spirit is able to cross. In this pagan part of the charm the magician is not a supplicant, he is a wielder of power and exultantly he exclaims: 'A victory charm I sing, a victory rod I bear, word-victory, work-victory'(6–7).

The Christian invocations that make up the greater part of the charm have caused the subjunctive-optative forms of the verbs in lines 7b–9: 'May they avail me; | that no mere obstruct me, nor foe oppress me, | nor my life turn to terror.' All the rest of the charm (10–30) is in this strain. It entreats, implores, and owes its effect to religious convictions. Thus armed, the man can safely undertake the journey, for no fiend will be able to harm him. As a friend of the saints and living in the peace of the Lord, he is secure against the Evil One who seeks his life.

The general meaning and purpose of the charm 'Against a Wen' are simple and straightforward. It is a cure against *wens*. In order to make them disappear a threat is uttered against the disease spirit, stressing the annihilation of some object by its use, so that finally nothing of the *wen* itself will remain.

Although several lines reveal an alliterative pattern, there is no metrical regularity, and the poetic and magic force of the charm lies not so much in the repetition of certain sounds as in that of parallel lines (2–3, 6–7, 8-10, 11–end).

It is striking that all four instances repeat the same idea in a triple form and that the only passage that does not show this form is obscure (4–5).

The magician begins by addressing the *wen*. On the third occasion he uses the diminutive '*wen* chicken', or, 'little *wen*', to impress it with the fact that he is its master, that its power is insignificant compared with his and that it will soon be destroyed. He scorns the power of a chicken or spirit (1), and goes on at once to tell the *wen* that it cannot stay in the patient any longer (2); it must stop its activity and leave for a hill where it will meet a brother (3–4). The amulet which is applied here consists of a leaf containing objects taken from a wolf and an eagle (5–7). Another possible explanation of lines 6–7 is that the sick spot is stroked by an eagle's feather and a wolf's claw and paw. In either case the idea is that by the attacks of these wild and ferocious animals the spirit is chased away or destroyed, and that gradually the effects of the disease will diminish and finally disappear (8–end). The first explanation is more likely because it accounts for the leaf put on the tumour. It is not essential that the amulet should contain the whole paw and claw; a small part is sufficient to represent the beast and the bird.

The magician's threat that the disease spirit will wither is elaborated in a number of fine comparisons: as a piece of coal burns to dust in the hearth, as dung shrinks on a wall, as water evaporates in a pail. It will become as small as a linseed grain, as the hipbone of a handworm, until it eventually sinks into nothingness.

Line 5 indicates that the *wen* was on the head.

Beowulf

The Tale of Sigemund (874b–97)

welhwylc gecwæð,
875 þæt he fram Sigemunde[s]¹ secgan hyrde
ellendædum, uncuþes fela,
Wælsinges² gewin, wide siðas,
þara þe gumena bearn gearwe ne wiston,
fæhðe ond fyrena, buton Fitela³ mid hine,
880 þonne he swulces hwæt secgan wolde,
eam his nefan, swa hie a wæron
æt niða gehwam nydgesteallan;
hæfdon ealfela eotena cynnes
sweordum gesægd. Sigemunde gesprong
885 æfter deaðdæge dom unlytel,
syþðan wiges heard wyrm acwealde,
hordes hyrde; he under harne stan,
æþelinges bearn ana geneðde
frecne dæde, ne wæs him Fitela mid;
890 hwæþre him gesælde, ðæt þæt swurd þurhwod
wrætlicne wyrm, þæt hit on wealle ætstod,
dryhtlic iren; draca morðre swealt.
Hæfde aglæca elne gegongen,
þæt he beahhordes brucan moste
895 selfes dome; sæbat gehleod,
bær on bearm scipes beorhte frætwa,
Wælses eafera; wyrm hat gemealt.

The Tale of Sigemund (874b–97)

recounted all
875 he had heard said of Sigemund's[1]
many uncouth deeds of courage,
the Wælsing's[2] strife, wide wanderings,
of which the sons of men knew naught,
feuds and crimes, except Fitela[3] there,
880 to whom he would tell everything,
uncle to nephew, for they ever were
friends in need in every fight.
Many a tribe of giants they
had slain with swords. For Sigemund since
885 his death-day earned no little fame,
when, battle-hard, he quelled the Worm,
hoard's guardian; beneath hoar stone,
he, *ætheling*'s son, had ventured lone,
a daring deed; Fitela was not there;
890 yet it was granted him that that glaive struck
the wondrous Worm – so that into the wall
the splendid iron stuck; the dragon died.
The hero's courage had contrived
to let him relish the ring-hoard,
895 as he liked; he filled the sea-boat, bore
bright treasure into the ship's bosom,
he, Wæls's son. The hot Worm melted.

---

[1] Sigemund (also 884), son of Wæls; father and uncle of Fitela.
[2] Wælsing, son of Wæls, that is Sigemund.
[3] Fitela (also 889), son and nephew of Sigemund, the dragon-slayer.

The Tale of Finn (1066b–1159a)

Hroþgares[1] scop
æfter medobence   mænan scolde,
[be] Finnes[2] eaferum,   ða hie se fær begeat,
hæleð Healf-Dena,   Hnæf[3] Scyldinga
1070   in Freswæle[4]   feallan scolde.
   Ne huru Hildeburh[5]   herian þorfte
Eotena[6] treowe;   unsynnum wearð
beloren leofum   æt þam lindplegan
bearnum ond broðrum;   hie on gebyrd hruron
1075   gare wunde;   þæt wæs geomuru ides!
Nalles holinga   Hoces[7] dohtor
meotodsceaft bemearn,   syþðan morgen com,
ða heo under swegle   geseon meahte
morþorbealo maga,   þær he[o] ær mæste heold
1080   worolde wynne.   Wig ealle fornam
Finnes þegnas   nemne feaum anum,
þæt he ne mehte   on þæm meðelstede
wig Hengeste[8]   wiht gefeohtan,
ne þa wealafe   wige forþringan
1085   þeodnes ðegne;   ac hig him geþingo budon,
þæt hie him oðer flet   eal gerymdon,
heale ond heahsetl,   þæt hie healfre geweald
wi ð Eotena bearn   agan moston,
ond æt feohgyftum   Folcwaldan[9] sunu
1090   dogra gehwylce   Dene weorþode,
Hengestes heap   hringum wenede
efne swa swiðe   sincgestreonum
fættan goldes,   swa he Fresena cyn
on beorsele   byldan wolde.
1095   Ða hie getruwedon   on twa healfa
fæste frioðuwære.   Fin Hengeste
elne unflitme   aðum benemde,
þæt he þa wealafe   weotena dome
arum heolde,   þæt ðær ænig mon

The Tale of Finn (1066b–1159a)

Hrothgar's[1] *scop*
upon the mead-benches should tell:
Finn's[2] followers when sudden woe befell them,
Hnæf[3] of the Scyldings, the Half-Danes' hero,
1070 was fated to fall on the Frisian[4] field.
No need had Hildeburh[5] indeed to praise
the Jutes'[6] good faith; blameless, she was
deprived of her dear ones at the shield-play:
son and brother fell to their fate
1075 wounded by spears; a sad woman that.
Not without reason did Hoc's[7] daughter
mourn destiny's decree, when morning came
and she could see, beneath the sky,
the slaughter of kinsmen. Where once she held
1080 most joy in the world, the war took all
Finn's *thanes*, save only a few,
so that he could not on the field
fight with Hengest[8] at all
nor guard the survivors by stirring against
1085 the prince's *thane*; but they offered in truce
to provide for them another place,
hall and high-seat, and half the rights
to share with the sons of the Jutes;
that Folcwalda's[9] son, at the gift-giving,
1090 every day should honour the Danes,
grant treasure to Hengest's troop,
even as much precious wealth
in plated gold as the Frisian's kin
would be glad to get in the beer-hall.
1095 Then they confirmed on either side
the firm peace-compact. To Hengest, Finn swore
solemn oaths, declared, unfeigned, that those
surviving the fight, with his *witan's* advice,
he would hold in honour so that no man

1100 wordum ne worcum wære ne bræce,
ne þurh inwitsearo æfre gemænden,
ðeah hie hira beaggyfan banan folgedon
ðeodenlease, þa him swa geþearfod wæs;
gyf þonne Frysna hwylc frecnan spræce
1105 ðæs morþorhetes myndgiend wære,
þonne hit sweordes ecg seðan scolde. –
Ad wæs geæfned, ond icge gold
ahæfen of horde. Here-Scyldinga
betst beadorinca wæs on bæl gearu.
1110 Æt þæm ade wæs eþgesyne
swatfah syrce, swyn ealgylden,
eofer irenheard, æþeling manig
wundum awyrded; sume on wæle crungon!
Het ða Hildeburh æt Hnæfes ade
1115 hire selfre sunu sweoloðe befæstan,
banfatu bærnan, ond on bæl don
eame on eaxle. Ides gnornode,
geomrode giddum. Guðrinc astah.
Wand to wolcnum wælfyra mæst,
1120 hlynode for hlawe; hafelan multon,
bengeato burston, ðonne blod ætspranc,
laðbite lices. Lig ealle forswealg,
gæsta gifrost, þara ðe þær guð fornam
bega folces; wæs hira blæd scacen.
1125 Gewiton him ða wigend wica neosian
freondum befeallen, Frysland[10] geseon,
hamas ond heaburh. Hengest ða gyt
wælfagne winter wunode mid Finne
[ea]l unhlitme; eard gemunde,
1130 þeah þe ne meahte on mere drifan
hringedstefnan, – holm storme weol,
won wið winde, winter yþe beleac
isgebinde, oþ ðæt oþer com
gear in geardas, – swa nu gyt deð,
1135 þa ðe syngales sele bewitiað,
wuldortorhtan weder. Ða wæs winter scacen,

1100 by word or deed should break the truce,
nor for malice ever mention that,
lordless, their prince's slayer, they
followed, now need forced them to it.
If, with rash speech, a Frisian should
1105 revive the reason for that hate
then sword's edge should settle it.
Funeral pyre prepared, piled gold raised
from hoard, the war-Scyldings' best
of heroes was made ready on the pyre.
1110 At the fire were easily seen
blood-stained battle-shirt, golden boar-crest,
iron-hard swine, many an *ætheling*
weary with wounds; some in battle fell.
Then Hildeburh on Hnæf's bier bade
1115 them yield her own son to the flames,
burn his body, place him on the fire,
at his uncle's shoulder. The woman mourned,
grieved, lamented loud. The warrior went up.
The greatest of death-fires to the welkin wound,
1120 roared before the barrow. Heads dissolved,
wounds gaped wide, as blood sprang out,
body's hate-bites. Fire swallowed up –
greediest of spirits – those slain in war
on both sides; shaken was their strength.
1125   The warriors departed to their dwellings,
lacking friends, to look on Friesland's[10]
homes and high-city. Hengest still stayed on
with Finn; through a winter, slaughter-stained,
all desolate, he dreamed about his land,
1130 though over the wave he could not drive
his ring-prowed ship; storms stirred the sea,
strove with the wind; winter locked the waves
in icy bonds – until there came another year
to men's dwellings, as it still does,
1135 ever biding its time,
glorious bright weather. Then was winter gone,

fæger foldan bearm;   fundode wrecca,
gist of geardum;   he to gyrnwræce
swiðor þohte   þonne to sælade,
1140   gif he torngemot   þurhteon mihte,
þæt he Eotena bearn   irne gemunde.
Swa he ne forwyrnde   w[e]orodrædende,
þonne him Hunlafing[11]   hildeleoman,
billa selest   on bearm dyde;
1145   þæs wæron mid Eotenum   ecge cuðe.
Swylce ferhðfrecan   Fin eft begeat
sweordbealo sliðen   æt his selfes ham,
siþðan grimne gripe   Guðlaf ond Oslaf[12]
æfter sæsiðe   sorge mændon,
1150   ætwiton weana dæl;   ne meahte wæfre mod
forhabban in hreþre.   Ða wæs heal roden
feonda feorum,   swilce Fin slægen,
cyning on corþre,   ond seo cwen numen.
Sceotend Scyldinga   to scypon feredon
1155   eal ingesteald   eorðcyninges,
swylce hie æt Finnes ham   findan meahton
sigla searogimma.   Hie on sælade
drihtlice wif   to Denum feredon,
læddon to leodum.

54

earth's lap fair, the exile eager to depart,
the guest from the dwellings; yet, vengeance for
his wrongs he thought on more than that sea-voyage –
1140 how he might foment discord
to settle the sons of the Jutes.
So he did not decline his duty when
Hunlaf's[11] son placed Battle-Bright,
the best of blades, upon his lap:
1145 its edges were known to the Jutes.
Thus to the war-wild Finn in his turn, too,
cruel sword-evil came to his home,
when Guthlaf and Oslaf[12] complained of grim onslaught
and sorrow subsequent to the sea-voyage,
1150 blamed him for their woes; the breast cannot hold
a restless heart. Then was hall reddened
with bodies of foes, Finn slain,
the king with his men, and the queen taken.
The Scylding warriors bore to the ship
1155 all the hall-trappings of the land's king,
whatsoever they could find at Finn's
of torques, precious gems. On the sea-track
they brought the lady back to the Danes,
led her to her people.

---

[1] Hrothgar, son of Heafldene, builder of Heorot.
[2] Finn (also 1081, 1096, 1128, 1146, 1152, 1156), king of the East Frisians
and also the Jutes; son of Folcwalda; married to Hildeburh, a Half-Dane.
[3] Hnæf (also 1114), leader of the Half-Danes, killed at Finnsburh by the
Frisians. Scylding (also 1108, 1154) a descendant or follower of Scyld, that
is, a Dane. Half-Danes, a Danish tribe to which Hoc, Hnæf and Hildeburh
belonged.
[4] Frisians (also 1104), a Germanic tribe whose language is closer to English
than other Low German dialects.
[5] Hildeburh (also 1114), Finn's Queen of Friesland, daughter of Hoc the Half-
Dane, sister of Hnæf.
[6] Jutes (also 1141), followers of Finn and the Frisians.
[7] Hoc, king of the Half-Danes, father of Hnæf and Hildeburh.
[8] Hengest (also 1091, 1096, 1127), a Half-Dane who succeeded Hnæf to the
leadership after the Frisian attack on the hall at Finnsburh.
[9] Folcwalda, father of Finn, the Frisian.

[10] Friesland, land of the Fri(e)sians. In the East, Finn's Kingdom; in the West, allied with the Franks against Hygelac.

[11] Hunlaf, probably the father of Guthlaf and Oslaf. *Battle-Bright*, according to the Anglo-Saxon poet is a famous sword, 'best of battle-blades', and, like *Hrunting* and *Nægling* (*Beowulf* 1490 and 2680), or *Mimming* (*Waldere*, I, 3) belongs to Germanic story.

[12] It is not clear from the poem whether Guthlaf and Oslaf were the sons of Hunlaf or merely followers of Hnæf.

The Tale of Thryth (1931b–62)

     Modþryðo[1] wæg,
fremu folces cwen, firen ondrysne;
nænig þæt dorste deor geneþan
swæsra gesiða, nefne sinfrea,
1935 þæt hire an dæges eagum starede;
ac him wælbende weotode tealde
handgewriþene; hraþe seoþðan wæs
æfter mundgripe mece geþinged,
þæt hit sceadenmæl scyran moste,
1940 cwealmbealu cyðan. Ne bið swylc cwenlic þeaw
idese to efnanne, þeah ðe hio ænlicu sy,
þætte freoðuwebbe feores onsæce
æfter ligetorne leofne mannan.
Huru þæt onhohsnod[e] Hemminges[2] mæg:
1945 ealodrincende oðer sædan,
þæt hio leodbealewa læs gefremede,
inwitniða, syððan ærest wearð
gyfen goldhroden geongum cempan,
æðelum diore, syððan hio Offan[3] flet
1950 ofer fealone flod be fæder lare
siðe gesohte; ðær hio syððan well
in gumstole, gode mære,
lifgesceafta lifigende breac,
hiold heahlufan wið hæleþa brego,
1955 ealles moncynnes mine gefræge
þone selestan bi sæm tweonum,
eormencynnes; forðam Offa wæs
geofum ond guðum, garcene man,
wide geweorðod, wisdome heold
1960 eðel sinne; – þonon Eomer[4] woc
hæleðum to helpe, Hem[m]inges mæg,
nefa Garmundes,[5] niða cræftig.

58

The Tale of Thryth (1931b-62)

(Mod)thryth,[1]
mighty queen, committed cruel crimes;
none so rash among her royal retinue
dared venture, save her lord, to set
1935 his eyes upon her openly by day;
but he might count on deadly bonds,
arresting hands; soon after seizure then
was sword summoned to settle,
patterned blade appointed to proclaim,
1940 death's doom. No queenly custom that
for wife to practise, peerless though she be,
that a loved liegeman's life-blood
a peace-weaver seek for pretended wrong.
But, Hemming's[2] kinsman hindered that.
1945 Then men at their ale told another tale:
how she burdened her folk with fewer ills,
less spiteful vengeance, after she
was given, gold-laden, to the young hero,
the beloved noble, when she sought
1950 Offa's[3] hall at her father's behest
over the fallow flood. Fame she found
there for generous gifts from the throne,
that she, while alive, used her fortune well;
held high love for the heroes' lord,
1955 of all mankind, as I have heard,
the best between the seas
of the races of men; so, Offa was
for wars and gifts, a spear-bold man,
widely honoured; he, in wisdom held
1960 his native land. Thence Eormær[4] sprang,
help of heroes, Hemming's kinsman,
Garmund's[5] grandson, mighty in the fray.

---

[1] (Mod)thryth, wife of the Anglian king Offa.

[2] Hemming (also 1961), an Angle, kinsman of Offa and Eomer (or Eormær).

[3] Offa (also 1956), king of the Continental Angles.

[4] Eomer, Anglian prince, son of Offa, grandson of Garmund, and kinsman of Hemming.

[5] Garmund, father of the Anglian king Offa.

The Tale of Freawaru (2024b–69a)

Sio gehaten (is),
2025 geong goldhroden, gladum suna Frodan;[1]
(h)afað þæs geworden wine Scyldinga,[2]
rices hyrde, ond þæt ræd talað,
þæt he mid ðy wife wælfæhða dæl,
sæcca gesette. Oft seldan hwær
2030 æfter leodhryre lytle hwile
bongar bugeð, þeah seo bryd duge!
Mæg þæs þonne ofþyncan ðeodne Heaðo-Beardna[3]
ond þegna gehwam þara leoda,
þonne he mid fæmnan on flett gæð:
2035 dryhtbearn Dena, duguða biwenede;
on him gladiað gomelra lafe,
heard ond hringmæl Heaða-Bear[d]na gestreon,
þenden hie ðam wæpnum wealdan moston, –
oð ðæt hie forlæddan to ðam lindplegan
2040 swæse gesiðas ond hyra sylfra feorh.
Þonne cwið æt beore se ðe beah gesyhð,
eald æscwiga, se ðe eall gem(an),
garcwealm gumena – him bið grim sefa –,
onginneð geomormod geong(um) cempan
2045 þurh hreðra gehygd higes cunnian,
wigbealu weccean, ond þæt word acwyð:
'Meaht ðu, min wine, mece gecnawan,
þone þin fæder to gefeohte bær
under heregriman hindeman siðe,
2050 dyre iren, þær hyne Dene slogon,
weoldon wælstowe, syððan Wiðergyld læg,[4]
æfter hæleþa hryre, hwate Scyldungas?
Nu her þara banena byre nathwylces
frætwum hremig on flet gæð,
2055 morðres gylpeð, ond þone maððum byreð,
þone þe ðu mid rihte rædan sceoldest.'
Manað swa ond myndgað mæla gehwylce

The Tale of Freawaru (2024b-69a)

Young and gold-adorned,
2025 she is betrothed to Froda's[1] fair son.
This had seemed good to the Scyldings'[2] lord,
the kingdom's protector, – he counts it prudent –
by means of this maiden that he may resolve
deadly feuds and fighting. Yet it is seldom
2030 the cruel spear lingers even a little,
after the prince's fall, despite a fair bride.
   This may displease the Heathobard[3] prince
and every noble among his nation,
when he walks with the woman into the hall:
2035 the highborn Danes, her retinue feasted;
on them flash heirlooms of their forbears,
hard, wave-patterned, Heathobard treasure –
theirs while they could wield those weapons,
ere they had led to destruction in shield-play
2040 their dear companions and their own lives.
Then at the beer an aged spearsman,
who eyes a ring-hilt, remembers it all,
the spear-death of heroes. His heart is grim.
And in gloomy mood he begins to test
2045 a young man's temper by musings of his mind.
To rouse accursed strife, he speaks these words:
'Canst thou, my friend, discern the blade,
the priceless iron, that thy father bore
to battle, helmed for his last fight;
2050 the Danes slew him, the hardy Scyldings took
possession of the field, when Withergyld[4]
perished, after the warriors' fall?
Here, now, one of his slayers' sons
walks in our hall, proud of that weapon,
2055 gloating in his gear, – boasts of his murder,
bearing the treasure thou shouldst rightly own.'
So, time and again, he prompts and provokes

sarum wordum,   oð ðæt sæl cymeð,
þæt se fæmnan þegn   fore fæder dædum
2060   æfter billes bite   blodfag swefeð,
ealdres scyldig;   him se oðer þonan
losað (li)figende,   con him land geare.
Þonne bioð (ab)rocene   on ba healfe
aðsweord eorla;   (syð)ðan Ingelde[5]
2065   weallað wælniðas,   ond him wiflufan
æfter cearwælmum   colran weorðað.
Þy ic Heaðo-Bear[d]na   hyldo ne telge,
dryhtsibbe dæl   Denum unfæcne,
freondscipe fæstne.

with wounding words, till the hour comes
that the lady's *thane*, for his father's deeds,
2060 from the bite of steel lies drenched in blood,
forfeit of life; the other thence
escapes alive – knows the country well.
On both sides then there will be broken
the oaths *eorls* swore; in Ingeld[5] surge
2065 deadly hate, and the love for his wife
grow cooler with the drifts of care.
Hence, I hold hollow the Heathobards'
lordly alliance with loyal Danes,
a specious friendship.

---

[1] Froda (or Frotho), King of Denmark, father of Ingeld the husband of Freawaru.

[2] Scyldings, see 'Tale of Finn' (1154), above.

[3] Heathobard (also 2037, 2066), a Germanic tribe whose king was Ingeld.

[4] Withergyld, a Heathobard warrior.

5 Ingeld, son of Froda, king of the Heathobards; married Freawaru, Hrothgar's daughter.

The Battle of Ravenswood & Death of Ongentheow (2922–98)

Ne ic te Sweoðeode sibbe oððe treowe
wihte ne wene, ac wæs wide cuð,
þætte Ongenðio[1] ealdre besnyðede
2925 Hæðcen[2] Hreþling wið Hrefnawudu,[3]
þa for onmedlan ærest gesohton
Geata leode Guð-Scilfingas.[4]
Sona him se froda fæder Ohtheres,[5]
eald ond egesfull ondslyht ageaf,
2930 abreot brimwisan, bryd ahredde,
gomela iomeowlan golde berofene,
Onelan[6] modor ond Ohtheres;
ond ða folgode feorhgeniðlan,
oð ðæt hi oðeodon earfoðlice
2935 in Hrefnesholt hlafordlease.
Besæt ða sinherge sweorda lafe
wundum werge; wean oft gehet
earmre teohhe ondlonge niht,
cwæð, he on mergenne meces ecgum
2940 getan wolde, sum[e] on galgtreowu[m]
[fuglum] to gamene. Frofor eft gelamp
sarigmodum somod ærdæge,
syððan hie Hygelaces[7] horn ond byman,
gealdor ongeaton, þa se goda com
2945 leoda dugoðe on last faran.
    Wæs sio swatswaðu Sw[e]ona ond Geata,
wælræs weora wide gesyne,
hu ða folc mid him fæhðe towehton.
Gewat him ða se goda mid his gædelingum,
2950 frod felageomor fæsten secean,
eorl Ongenþio ufor oncirde;
hæfde Higelaces hilde gefrunen,
wlonces wigcræft; wiðres ne truwode,
þæt he sæmannum onsacan mihte,

66

The Battle of Ravenswood & Death of Ongentheow (2922-98)

Nor in the least do I expect peace
or trust from the Swedish folk;
for it is widely known that Ongentheow[1]
2925 took the life of Hæthcyn,[2] Hrethel's son,
near Ravenswood[3] when the Geatish folk
first proudly attacked the War-Scylfings.[4]
Straightway Ohthere's[5] wary sire,
aged and awesome, made a counter-thrust,
2930 cut down the sea-king, rescued his consort,
now an old woman, bereft of her gold,
Onela's[6] mother and Ohthere's;
then he pursued his mortal foes
until they escaped him painfully,
2935 lordless, into Ravenswood.
With a great army he beset those still
sword-spared, wound-weary, often vowed woes
to the ill-omened troop the whole night through,
said in the morn that he would cut down
2940 some with sword-edges, hang some on gallows-trees
as sport for birds. Relief came then
to the sad-hearted together at dawn,
with Hygelac's[7] horn and trumpet blast,
when they saw the good man bear down on their track,
2945 with a body of his own retinue.
    The bloody track of Swedes and Geats,
the slaughter-strife of men, was widely seen, –
how these folk fostered the feud between them.
Then the good king, went with his kinsmen,
2950 old and great-griefed, to seek his stronghold.
The *eorl* Ongentheow moved farther off.
He had heard of Hygelac's prowess in war,
proud battle-craft: he doubted his defence,
doubted his skill to fight off the sea-folk,

2955 heaðoliðendum hord forstandan,
bearn ond bryde; beah eft þonan
eald under eorðweall. Þa wæs æht boden
Sweona leodum, segn Higelace[s]
freoðowong þone forð ofereodon,
2960 syððan Hreðlingas to hagan þrungon.
Þær wearð Ongenðiow ecgum sweorda,
blondenfexa on bid wrecen,
þæt se þeodcyning ðafian sceolde
Eafores[8] anne dom. Hyne yrringa
2965 Wulf[9] Wonreding wæpne geræhte,
þæt him for swenge swat ædrum sprong
forð under fexe. Næs he forht swa ðeh,
gomela Scilfing, ac forgeald hraðe
wyrsan wrixle wælhlem þone,
2970 syððan ðeodcyning þyder oncirde.
Ne meahte se snella sunu Wonredes
ealdum ceorle ondslyht giofan,
ac he him on heafde helm ær gescer,
þæt he blode fah bugan sceolde,
2975 feoll on foldan; næs he fæge þa git,
ac he hyne gewyrpte, þeah ðe him wund hrine.
Let se hearda Higelaces þegn
brad[n]e mece, þa his broðor læg,
ealdsweord eotonisc entiscne helm
2980 brecan ofer bordweal; ða gebeah cyning,
folces hyrde, wæs in feorh dropen.
Ða wæron monige, þe his mæg wriðon,
ricone arærdon, ða him gerymed wearð,
þæt hie wælstowe wealdan moston.
2985 Þenden reafode rinc oðerne,
nam on Ongenðio irenbyrnan,
heard swyrd hilted, ond his helm somod;
hares hyrste Higelace bær.
He ð(am) frætwum feng ond him fægre gehet
2990 leana (mid) leodum, ond gelæste swa;
geald þone guðræs Geata dryhten,

2955 from the seafaring host to safeguard his hoard,
his children and wife. But the old man drew back
behind his earth-wall. Then chase was given
to the Swedish folk, and Hygelac's standards
flew over the fortress
2960 as Hrethel's retainers thronged the citadel.
There was the grizzled head, Ongentheow,
brought to bay by the blades of swords,
the people's king compelled to yield
to Eofor's[8] hands alone. Wulf,[9] Wonred's son,
2965 struck with his blade in wrath, so that the blood
from the blow sprang streaming out of his veins
under his hair. But, unafraid still,
the aged Scylfing speedily repaid
that savage stroke with savager return,
2970 when the people's king turned towards him.
Wonred's active son could not return
the blow the older man had given him,
which split the helmet first upon his head,
forcing him to sink down, stained with blood.
2975 He fell to earth; he was not doomed yet,
but he came round, though the wound pained him.
Then Hygelac's hardy follower let
his giant-forged steel, his broad blade, break
the massive helmet, across the shield-wall
2980 when his brother lay dead; then the king fell,
the keeper of folk, mortally struck.
Many were there who bound up his brother,
raised him up quickly, when they were granted
success on the slaughter-field.
2985 Then a warrior stripped the other,
took from Ongentheow his iron mail,
his hard-hilted sword and his helmet too;
bore the hoary one's harness to Hygelac.
He took that treasure and promised him fairly
2990 rewards among men; and fulfilled his pledge;
the lord of the Geats, he, Hrethel's son,

Hreðles eafora,   þa he to ham becom,
Iofore ond Wulfe   mid ofermaðmum,
sealde hiora gehwæðrum   hund þusenda
2995 landes ond locenra beaga, – ne ðorfte him ða lean oðwitan
mon on middangearde,   syðða[n] hie ða mærða geslogon;
ond ða Iofore forgeaf   angan dohtor,
hamweorðunge,   hyldo to wedde.

on his return home gave battle-reward
to Eofor and Wulf, much treasure:
to each a hundred thousandworth
2995 in land and linked rings, – for those gifts none need
have reason to reproach him, since they were earned
as honours in war; – and to Eofor, his daughter
in token of friendship, a fair thing for his home.

1 Ongentheow (also 2952, 2961, 2986), Swedish king, father of Ohthere and Onela; slain by Eofor, a Geat.
2 Hæthcyn, second son of Hrethel; he accidentally shot his brother, Herebald. Hrethel, king of the Geats; father of Hygelac; Beowulf's maternal grandfather.
3 *Hrefnesholt* [Ravenswood] (also 2935), where the Swedes were decisively defeated by the Geats under Hygelac in 510 and made peace with them. The Geats (also 2991), a tribe in Southern Sweden, Beowulf's people.
4 Scylfing, Swedish royal family, in the plural the Swedes.
5 Ohthere (also 2932), elder son of Ongentheow, king of Sweden; father of Eanmund and Eadgils; brother of Onela.
6 Onela, younger son of Ongentheow, the Swedish king; married Hrothgar's sister; killed by Eadgils.
7 Hygelac (also 2952, 2958, 2978, 2988), maternal uncle of Beowulf.
8 Eofor (also 2993, 2997), Geatish warrior, son of Wonred and brother of Wulf; slayer of the Swedish king Ongentheow, and rewarded with marriage to Hygelac's daughter. Wulf (also 2993), son of Wonred; fought Ongentheow. Wonred (also 2971), a Geat, father of Eofor and Wulf.
9 Wulf (also 2993), son of Wonred; fought Ongentheow. Wonred (also 2971), a Geat, father of Eofor and Wulf.

71

The Finnsburh Fragment

The Finnsburh Fragment

.... (hor)nas byrnað.'
[H]næf[1] hleoþrode ða heaþogeong cyning:
'Ne ðis ne dagað eastan, ne her draca ne fleogeð,
ne her ðisse healle, hornas ne byrnað;
5 ac her forþ berað, fugelas singað,
gylleð græghama, guðwudu hlynneð,
scyld scefte oncwyð. Nu scyneð þes mona
waðol under wolcnum; nu arisað weadæda,
ðe ðisne folces nið fremman willað.
10 Ac onwacnigeað nu, wigend mine,
habbað eowre linda, hicgeaþ on ellen,
winnað on orde, wesað on mode!'
    Ða aras mænig goldhladen ðegn, gyrde hine his swurde;
ða to dura eodon drihtlice cempan,
15 Sigeferð[2] and Eaha, hyra sword getugon,
and æt oþrum durum Ordlaf and Guþlaf,[3]
and Hengest[4] sylf, hwearf him on laste.
Ða gyt Garulf[e] Guðere[5] styrde,
ðæt he swa freolic feorh forman siþe
20 to ðære healle durum hyrsta ne bære,
nu hyt niþa heard anyman wolde;
ac he frægn ofer eal undearninga,
deormod hæleþ, hwa ða duru heolde.
'Sigeferþ is min nama (cweþ he), ic eom Secgena leod,
25 wreccea wide cuð; fæla ic weana gebad,
heordra hilda; ðe is gyt her witod,
swæþer ðu sylf to me secean wylle.'
    Ða wæs on healle wælslihta gehlyn,
sceolde cellod bord cenum on handa,
30 banhelm berstan, buruhðelu dynede, –
oð æt ðære guðe Garulf gecrang
ealra ærest eorðbuendra,
Guðlafes[6] sunu, ymbe hyne godra fæla,
hwearflicra hræw. Hræfen wandrode

The Finnsburh Fragment

.... gables burn!'
Hnæf,[1] the battle-crazed young king, replied:
'No eastern dawn is this, not here does dragon fly,
nor here do this hall's gables burn;
5 but war's afoot here, carrion fowl shall sing,
grey-coat howl, war-wood resound,
shield echo shaft. Now shines the moon,
through scudding cloud; now dire deeds rise
will stir this folk to bitter strife.
10 But, warriors mine, awake ye now,
secure your shields, consider courage well,
strive in the forefront, be of firm resolve!'
    Many a gold-lade thane then, springing up, girt on his sword;
and, to the door, the doughty champions strode,
15 Sigeferth[2] and Eaha, drawing swords;
Ordlaf and Guthlaf[3] to the other doors,
with Hengest[4] himself hard on their heels.
Garulf again urged Guthere[5]
in that first onset not so freely
20 to hazard his life at that hall's doors,
where battle-bold heroes would reave him of it;
but the fearless hero, for all to hear,
called to know who held the door.
'My name is Sigeferth (said he), prince of the Secgas,
25 a widely-known wanderer; many blows have I borne
in fierce fights; yet here is decreed
whatever thou wilt thyself seek of me.'
    Then was there sound of slaughter in hall;
bold hands grasped their hollow shields,
30 bone-helms burst, the hall-floor rang
till Garulf fell in that affray,
of all men first,
Guthlaf's[6] son, many good ones about him,
corpses brave. The raven circled round,

75

35   sweart and sealobrun.   Swurdleoma stod,
     swylce eal Finnsburuh [7] fyrenu wære.
     Ne gefrægn ic næfre wurþlicor   æt wera hilde
     sixtig sigebeorna   sel gebæran,
     ne nefre swanas hwitne medo   sel forgyldan,
40   ðonne Hnæfe guldan   his hægstealdas.
        Hig fuhton fif dagas,   swa hyra nan ne feol,
     drihtgesiða,   ac hig ða duru heoldon.
     Ða gewat him wund hæleð   on wæg gangan,
     sæde þæt his byrne   abrocen wære,
45   heresceorp unhror,   and eac wæs his helm ðyr[e]l.
     Ða hine sona frægn   folces hyrde,
     hu ða wigend hyra   wunda genæson,
     oððe hwæþer ðæra hyssa ....

35 swart and sallow. The sword-flash gleamed,
as if all Finnsburh[7] were aflame.
Never have I heard of worthier warriors,
of sixty fighters better bearing arms,
nor finer recompense in mead to heroes paid
40 than Hnæf to his young gallants gave.
   Five days they fought, yet none fell there,
noble comrades, but they held the doors.
A wounded warrior sped him on his way,
declared his *byrny* now was broken through,
45 his war-dress weak, his helmet pierced too.
The prince of the people enquired of him
how well the warriors endured their wounds,
or which of the youths ....

[1] Hnæf (also 40), see 'The Tale of Finn' (1069), above.
[2] Sigeferth (also 24), a Secgan, one of Hnæf's warriors. Eaha, a Danish warrior.
[3] Ordlaf and Guthlaf, Danes.
[4] Hengest, see 'The Tale of Finn' (1083), above.
[5] Garulf and Guthhere, Frisians.
[6] Guthlaf, a Frisian, father of Garulf.
[7] Finnsburh, Finn's capital in Friesland.

Waldere

Waldere

I

[..........] hyrde hyne georne:
'Huru Welande(s)[1]   worc ne geswiceð
monna ænigum   ðara ðe Mimming[2] can
hear[d]ne gehealdan;   oft æt hilde gedreas
5   swatfag ond sweordwund   sec[g] æfter oðrum.
Ætlan[3] ordwyga,   ne læt ðin ellen nu gyt
gedreosan to dæge,   dryhtscipe .....
[..........]   (Nu) is se dæg cumen,
þæt ðu scealt aninga   oðer twega,
10   lif forleosan,   oððe lang[n]e dom
agan mid eldum,   Ælfheres[4] sunu!
Nalles ic ðe, wine min,   wordum cide,
ðy ic ðe gesawe   æt ðam sweordplegan
ðurh edwitscype   æniges monnes
15   wig forbugan,   oððe on weal fleon,
lice beorgan,   ðeah þe laðra fela
ðinne byrnhomon   billum heowun;
ac ðu symle furðor   feohtan sohtest,
mæl ofer mearce;   ðy ic ðe metod ondred,
20   þæt ðu to fyrenlice   feohtan sohtest
æt ðam ætstealle,   oðres monnes
wigrædenne.   Weorða ðe selfne
godum dædum,   ðenden ðin God recce!
Ne murn ðu for ði mece;   ðe wearð maðma cyst
25   gifeðe to [g]eoce,   mid ðy ðu Guðhere[5] scealt
beot forbigan,   ðæs ðe he ðas beaduwe ongan
mid unryhte   ærest secan.
Forsoc he ðam swurde   ond ðam syncfatum,
beaga mænigo;   nu sceal beaga leas
30   hworfan from ðisse hilde,   hlafurd secan
ealdne eðel,   oððe her ær swefan,
gif he ða ....

Waldere

I

[..........] bravely urged him:
'Surely Welund's[1] work does not betray
any man who can hold Mimming[2] hard.
In the fray foes often fell
5 blood-stained, sword-struck, man after man.
Attila's[3] foremost spear, let not thy strength,
thy dignity, decline today.
[..........] Now is come the day
when, son of Ælfhere,[4] thou must achieve
10 among men, singly, either of two things:
forfeit life or gain eternal fame.
Never will I chide thee, friend, with words,
say I saw thee at the sword-play
shun, for shame, another man's
15 attack, or fly to the wall
to save thy life, though many foes
hacked at thy *byrny* with blades.
But thou soughtst ever to press the fight
further; so, for thy fate I feared
20 that all too keenly thou shouldst seek
to meet upon the field another man
in war. Win fame for thyself
by good deeds, and may God guard thee the while!
Fear not for thy falchion – to thee the best blade
25 was given to aid us. With it Guthhere's[5]
boast thou shalt break since he began
unjustly first to seek the fray.
He scorned the sword and treasures,
many rings; now, ringless, he
30 must turn from this battle, seek his lord,
his ancient home, or die here before that,
if he then ....

[1] Welund, the famous smith of Germanic story, is mentioned in *Beowulf* (455) as having fashioned the armour of Hrethel, king of the Geats. *Deor* deals with his fate at Nithhad's court, and hints at his ultimate escape. The Franks Casket depicts two scenes from the Welund story.

[2] *Mimming* is one of the most famous swords of Germanic story, said to have been forged by Welund, although it is believed by some to have been the handiwork of Mimir the Smith. The sword belongs to Widia and how it reached Waldere is not known.

[3] Ætla (or Attila), king of the Huns (d. 453), the only non-Germanic personage who plays an important part in Germanic heroic song. Ostro-Germanic tradition makes him a generous prince, Frankish tradition a treacherous tyrant. Ætla is also mentioned in *Widsith* (19, 65).

[4] Ælfhere (also II, 18), father of Waldere. From his occurrence in *Waltharius* and *Walther* we may assume that he was a character in the original lay. In *Waldere* he is already dead since Waldere wears his armour. We do not know what his rôle may have been in the original lay.

[5] Guthhere (or Gundahari), king of the Burgundians, probably slain in the battle with the Huns in 436 or 437. Praised as a liberal king in *Widsith* (66 f.), his character is drawn less sympathetically in *Waltharius*. In the *Atlakviða* he is the ideal Germanic chief: proud, defiant, courageous.

II

'.......... [me]ce bæteran
buton ðam anum, ðe ic eac hafa,
on stanfate stille gehided.
  Ic wat þæt [h]it dohte Ðeodric[1] Widian
5 selfum onsendon, ond eac sinc micel
maðma mid ði mece, monig oðres mid him
golde gegirwan, iulean genam,
þæs ðe hine of nearwum Niðhades[2] mæg,
Welandes bearn, Widia[3] ut forlet,
10 ðurh fifela geweald forð onette.'
  Waldere[4] maðelode, wiga ellenrof –
hæfde him on handa hildefro[f]re,
guðbilla gripe, gyddode wordum:
'Hwæt, ðu huru wendest, wine Burgenda,[5]
15 þæt me Hagenan hand hilde gefremede
ond getwæmde feðewigges. Feta, gyf ðu dyrre,
æt ðus heaðuwerigan hare byrnan!
Standeð me her on eaxelum Ælfheres laf
god ond geapneb, golde geweorðod,
20 ealles unscende æðelinges reaf
to habbanne, þonne ha[n]d wereð
feorhhord feondum; ne bið fah wið me,
þonne (me) unmægas eft ongynnað,
mecum gemetað, swa ge me dydon.
25 Ðeah mæg sige syllan se ðe symle byð
recon ond rædfest ryhta gehwilces;
se ðe him to ðam halgan helpe gelifeð,
to Gode gioce, he þær gearo findeð,
gif ða earnunga ær geðenceð.
30 Þonne moten wlance welan britnian,
æhtum wealdan; þæt is .....'

II

'......... a better sword
except the one that I have also in
its stone-encrusted scabbard laid aside.
I know that Theodric[1] thought to Widia's self
5   to send it and much treasure too,
jewels with the blade, many more besides,
gold-geared; he received reward
when Nithhad's[2] kinsman, Widia,[3] Welund's son,
delivered him from durance;
10   through press of monsters hastened forth.'
     Waldere[4] boasted, warrior brave,
held his battle-help in hand,
biting war-blade, uttered words:
'Lo, thou didst truly think, Burgundian[5] lord,
15   that Hagen's hand would help to hinder me,
cut me down in combat. If thou darest, come and take
my hoary *byrny* from me who am battle-worn.
Ælfhere's heirloom lies upon my shoulders here,
good and woven-wide, adorned with gold,
20   not at all a mean garb for a prince
to have when his hand guards
his frame from fiends. It will not fail
me when unfriendly kinsmen make a fresh attack,
meet me with swords, as ye have done.
25   Yet may He grant me victory who is
ever prompt and wise in every righteous cause.
He who trusts him to the Holy One for help,
to God for aid, shall find it ready there,
if he takes prior thought of how to merit it.
30   Then may the proud dispose of wealth,
wield power, that is .....'

---

[1] Theodric of Verona (454-526), king of the Ostrogoths, Arian heretic, treacherous murderer of Odoaker (493), the last great Ostrogoth, after whose death the power of his people waned. In German song, Theodric becomes the greatest hero. He is one of the examples of misfortune outlived in *Deor* (18 f.).

2 Nithhad, according to *Waldere*, is the maternal grandfather of Widia. The name is probably of Saxon origin.

3 Widia (also, 4), the historic Gothic champion Vidigoia mentioned twice by Jordanes (ch. v, ch. xxxiv). In song he later became attached to Theodric. In *Widsith* (124, 130) he occurs as Wudga who, together with Hama, rules as an independent chief.

4 Waldere, for whom no historical prototype has been established, and whose place of origin is not indicated in the fragments, is placed by other sources west of the Rhine.

5 Burgendas, an East-Germanic tribe which founded a kingdom on the banks of the Rhine, whose power was broken in the fifth century by combined Gaulish and Hunnish hostility. Their fate, transformed into the personal tragedy of the ruling house, is reflected in the Eddic poems and the *Nibelungenlied*. The Burgundians are mentioned in *Widsith* (19, 65).

Widsith

Widsith

Widsið maðolade, wordhord onleac,
se þe monna mæst mægþa ofer eorþan,
folca geondferde; oft he on flette geþah
mynelicne maþþum. Him from Myrgingum[1]
5   æþele onwocon. He mid Ealhhilde,
fælre freoþuwebban, forman siþe
Hreðcyninges ham gesohte
eastan of Ongle, Eormanrices,[2]
wraþes wærlogan. Ongon þa worn sprecan:
10   'Fela ic monna gefrægn mægþum wealdan!
Sceal þeodna gehwylc þeawum lifgan,
eorl æfter oþrum eðle rædan,
se þe his þeodenstol geþeon wile.
Þara wæs Hwala hwile selast,
15   ond Alexandreas ealra ricost
monna cynnes, ond he mæst geþah
þara þe ic ofer foldan gefrægen hæbbe.
Ætla[3] weold Hunum, Eormanric Gotum,
Becca[4] Baningum, Burgendum Gifica.
20   Casere weold Creacum ond Cælic Finnum,
Hagena Holmrygum ond Heoden[5] Glommum.
Witta weold Swæfum, Wada[6] Hælsingum,
Meaca Myrgingum, Mearchealf Hundingum.
Þeodric[7] weold Froncum, Þyle Rondingum,
25   Breoca[8] Brondingum, Billing Wernum.
Oswine weold Eowum ond Ytum Gefwulf,
Fin[9] Folcwalding Fresna cynne.
Sigehere lengest Sædenum weold,
Hnæf[10] Hocingum, Helm Wulfingum,
30   Wald Woingum, Wod Þyringum,
Sæferð[11] Sycgum, Sweom Ongendþeow,[12]
Sceafthere Ymbrum, Sceafa Longbeardum,
Hun Hætwerum ond Holen Wrosnum.
Hringweald wæs haten Herefarena cyning.

Widsith

Widsith spoke, unlocked his word-hoard,
he, most travelled of men upon earth
among famous folk; in hall often took
splendid treasure. His forbears sprang
5   from the Myrging[1] tribe. Together with Ealhhild,
gracious peace-weaver, for the first time,
east out of Angeln, Eormanric's[2]
home he sought, that savage king,
fierce and faithless. He spoke at length:
10   'I have heard much of the rulers of men!
A lord ought to live by custom and law;
one *eorl* rule a realm after another,
who wishes his princely throne to thrive.
Of these was Hwala the best for a time,
15   and Alexander mightiest of all,
of the race of men, and he prospered most
of those I have heard about over the earth.
Ætla[3] ruled the Huns, Eormanric the Goths,
Becca[4] the Banings, Gifeca the Burgundians.
20   Caesar ruled the Greeks and Cælic the Finns,
Hagena the Island-Rugians and Heoden[5] the Gloms.
Witta ruled the Swabians, Wade[6] the Hælsings,
Meaca the Myrgings, Mearchalf the Hundings.
Theodric[7] ruled the Franks, Thyle the Rondings,
25   Breoca[8] the Brondings, Billing the Werns.
Oswine ruled the Eows, and Gefwulf the Jutes;
Fin[9] Folcwalding the tribe of the Frisians.
Sigehere ruled the Sea-Danes longest,
Hnæf[10] the Hocings, Helm the Wulfings,
30   Wald the Woings, Wod the Thuringians,
Sæferth[11] the Secgs, Ongentheow[12] the Swedes,
Sceafthere the Ymbers, Sceafa the Lombards,
Hun the Hætwars, and Holen the Wrosns.
The Raiders' king was called Hringweald.

35 Offa[13] weold Ongle, Alewih Denum;
   se wæs þara manna modgast ealra,
   no hwæþre he ofer Offan eorlscype fremede,
   ac Offa geslog ærest monna,
   cnihtwesende, cynerica mæst.
40 Nænig efeneald him eorlscipe maran
   onorette. Ana sweorde
   merce gemærde wið Myrgingum
   bi Fifeldore; heoldon forð siþþan
   Engle ond Swæfe, swa hit Offa geslog.
45 Hroþwulf ond Hroðgar[14] heoldon lengest
   sibbe ætsomne suhtorfædran,
   siþþan hy forwræcon Wicinga cynn
   ond Ingeldes ord forbigdan,
   forheowan æt Heorote Heaðobeardna þrym.
50 Swa ic geondferde fela fremdra londa
   geond ginne grund. Godes ond yfles
   þær ic cunnade cnosle bidæled,
   freomægum feor folgade wide.
   Forþon ic mæg singan ond secgan spell,
55 mænan fore mengo in meoduhealle
   hu me cynegode cystum dohten.
   Ic wæs mid Hunum ond mid Hreðgotum,
   mid Sweom ond mid Geatum ond mid Suþdenum.
   Mid Wenlum ic wæs ond mid Wærnum ond mid Wicingum.
60 Mid Gefþum ic wæs ond mid Winedum ond mid Gefflegum.
   Mid Englum ic wæs ond mid Swæfum ond mid Ænenum.
   Mid Seaxum ic wæs ond Sycgum ond mid Sweordwerum.
   Mid Hronum ic wæs ond mid Deanum ond mid Heaþoreamum.
   Mid Þyringum ic wæs ond mid Þrowendum,
65 ond mid Burgendum, þær ic beag geþah;
   me þær Guðhere[15] forgeaf glædlicne maþþum
   songes to leane. Næs þæt sæne cyning!
   Mid Froncum ic wæs ond mid Frysum ond mid Frumtingum.
   Mid Rugum ic wæs ond mid Glommum ond mid Rumwalum.
70 Swylce ic wæs on Eatule mid Ælfwine,[16]
   se hæfde moncynnes, mine gefræge,

35 Offa[13] ruled Angeln, Alewih the Danes:
 he was the bravest of all those men,
 but, in heroism, not better than Offa;
 for Offa was first among men to win
 by battle the greatest realm, while young.
40 No one at his age accomplished greater
 heroism. He, with his single sword,
 marked out the frontier with the Myrgings
 at Fifeldor. It was later held
 by Angles and Swabians, as Offa struck it.
45 Hrothwulf and Hrothgar[14] longest kept
 peace together, nephew and uncle,
 after they routed the Viking tribe,
 humbled Ingeld's vanguard and hewed
 down at Heorot the Heathobard host.
50 Thus I fared through many foreign lands,
 over the wide world. Weal and woe
 I suffered there, severed from family,
 far from free kinsmen, wandering widely.
 So I may sing and utter a measure;
55 recite before company in the mead hall
 how royal dispensers gave to me freely.
 I was with the Huns and with the Goths,
 with the Swedes and with the Geats and with the South-Danes.
 I was with the Wendels and with the Wærns and with the Vikings.
60 I was with the Gepids and with the Wends and with the Gefflegs.
 I was with the Angles and with the Swabians and with the Ænenes.
 I was with the Saxons and with the Secgs and with the Swordmen.
 I was with the Whalemen and with the Danes and the Heathoreams.
 I was with the Thuringians and with the men of Drontheim
65 and with the Burgundians where I took a torque;
 there Guthhere[15] gave me gleaming treasures
 in reward for my song; that was no sluggish king!
 I was with the Franks and with the Frisians and with the Frumtings.
 I was with the Rugians and with the Glomms and with the Romans.
70 I was also in Italy with Ælfwine,[16]
 Eadwine's son; I have heard that he,

leohteste hond   lofes to wyrcenne,
heortan unhneaweste   hringa gedales,
beorhtra beaga,   bearn Eadwines.
75 Mid Sercingum ic wæs   ond mid Seringum;
mid Creacum ic wæs ond mid Finnum   ond mid Casere,
se þe winburga   geweald ahte,
wiolena ond wilna,   ond Wala rices.
Mid Scottum ic wæs ond mid Peohtum   ond mid Scridefinnum;
80 mid Lidwicingum ic wæs ond mid Leonum   ond mid Longbeardum,
mid hæðnum ond mid hæleþum   ond mid Hundingum.
mid Israhelum ic wæs   ond mid Exsyringum,
mid Ebreum ond mid Indeum   ond mid Egyptum.
Mid Moidum ic wæs ond mid Persum   ond mid Myrgingum,
85 ond Mofdingum   ond ongend Myrgingum,
ond mid Amothingum.   Mid Eastþyringum ic wæs
ond mid Eolum ond mid Istum   ond Idumingum.
    Ond ic wæs mid Eormanrice   ealle þrage,
þær me Gotena cyning   gode dohte;
90 se me beag forgeaf,   burgwarena fruma,
on þam siex hund wæs   smætes goldes,
gescyred sceatta   scillingrime;
þone ic Eadgilse[17]   on æht sealde,
minum hleodryhtne,   þa ic to ham bicwom,
95 leofum to leane,   þæs þe he me lond forgeaf,
mines fæder eþel,   frea Myrginga.
Ond me þa Ealhhild   oþerne forgeaf,
dryhtcwen duguþe,   dohtor Eadwines.
Hyre lof lengde   geond lond fela,
100 þonne ic be songe   secgan sceolde
hwær ic under swegle   selast wisse
goldhrodene cwen   giefe bryttian.
Ðonne wit Scilling   sciran reorde
for uncrum sigedryhtne   song ahofan,
105 hlude bi hearpan   hleoþor swinsade,
þonne monige men,   modum wlonce,
wordum sprecan,   þa þe wel cuþan,
þæt hi næfre song   sellan ne hyrdon.

of all mankind, had the quickest hand
at gaining renown in giving out rings,
gleaming bracelets, a most generous heart.
75 I was with the Saracens and with the Seres.
I was with the Greeks and with the Finns and with Caesar,
who had festive cities in his power,
riches, treasures, and the realm of Wales.
I was with the Scots and with the Picts and with the Scridefinns.
80 I was with the Bretons and with the Leons and with the Lombards,
with the heathens and with the heroes, and with the Hundings.
I was with the Israelites and with the Assyrians,
with the Hebrews and with the Indians and with the Egyptians.
I was with the Medes and with the Persians and with the Myrgings,
85 and with the Mofdings, and against the Myrgings,
and with the Amothings. I was with the East-Thuringians
and with the Eols and with the Ests and with the Idumings.
     And I was with Eormanric all the time,
where the king of the Goths treated me graciously;
90 he, ruler of the cities, gave me a ring
in which there was reckoned to be six hundred
pieces of pure gold counted in shillings;
I gave that into the keeping of Eadgils,[17]
to my protector, when I came home,
95 as meed to the loved one, lord of the Myrgings,
for he granted me land, my father's estate.
And Eadwine's daughter, Ealhhild, a queen
noble in majesty, then gave me another.
Her praise was bruited through many lands,
100 when in song I had to tell
where under heaven I knew best
a gold-adorned queen grant gifts.
When Scilling and I with clear voice raised
the song before our victorious lord –
105 loud to the lyre our lay resounded –
then many men, proud of mind,
who knew well, declared in words
they never had heard a better song.

Đonan ic ealne geondhwearf eþel Gotena,
110 sohte ic a gesiþa þa selestan;
þæt wæs innweorud Earmanrices.
Heðcan sohte ic ond Beadecan ond Herelingas,
Emercan sohte ic ond Fridlan ond Eastgotan,[18]
frodne ond godne fæder Unwenes.
115 Seccan sohte ic ond Beccan, Seafolan ond Þeodric,[19]
Heaþoric ond Sifecan,[20] Hliþe ond Incgenþeow.[21]
Eadwine sohte ic ond Elsan, Ægelmund ond Hungar,
ond þa wloncan gedryht Wiþmyrginga.
Wulfhere sohte ic ond Wyrmhere; ful oft þær wig ne alæg,
120 þonne Hræda here heardum sweordum
ymb Wistlawudu wergan sceoldon
ealdne eþelstol Ætlan leodum.
Rædhere sohte ic ond Rondhere, Rumstan ond Gislhere,
Wiþergield ond Freoþeric,[22] Wudgan ond Haman;
125 ne wæran þæt gesiþa þa sæmestan,
þeah þe ic hy anihst nemnan sceolde.
Ful oft of þam heape hwinende fleag
giellende gar on grome þeode;
wræccan þær weoldan wundan golde
130 werum ond wifum, Wudga ond Hama.[23]
Swa ic þæt symle onfond on þære feringe,
þæt se biþ leofast londbuendum
se þe him god syleð gumena rice
to gehealdenne, þenden he her leofað.'
135 Swa scriþende gesceapum hweorfað
gleomen gumena geond grunda fela,
þearfe secgað, þoncword sprecaþ,
simle suð oþþe norð sumne gemetað
gydda gleawne, geofum unhneawne,
140 se þe fore duguþe wile dom aræran,
eorlscipe æfnan, oþþæt eal scæceð,
leoht ond lif somod; lof se gewyrceð,
hafað under heofonum heahfæstne dom.

Thence all through the land of the Goths
110 I fared; the best of comrades always sought,
such were the household of Eormanric.
I sought Hethca and Beadeca, and the Herelings.
I sought Emerca and Fridla, and East-Gota,[18]
the wise and good father of Unwen.
115 I sought Secca and Becca, Seafola and Theodric,[19]
Heathoric and Sifeca,[20] Hlithe and Incgentheow.[21]
I sought Eadwine and Elsa, Ægelmund and Hungar,
and the proud band of the Withmyrgings.
I sought Wulfhere and Wyrmhere: not often was there rest from war
120 when the Goths with strong swords
were forced to defend their ancient domain
against Attila's folk by Vistula-wood.
I sought Rædhere and Rondhere, Rumstan and Gislhere,
Withergield and Freotheric[22] and Wudga and Hama;
125 those were not the worst of comrades,
though I should name them last of all.
Full often from that band flew screaming,
the whistling spear against hostile hosts;
there Wudga and Hama,[23] wanderers, had sway
130 over men and women with twisted gold.
So I have always found it in my wayfaring
that he is dearest to land-dwellers
to whom God grants dominion over men
to hold as long as he lives here.'
135 Roving thus, as is their destiny,
men's minstrels wander over many lands;
they tell their need, speak words of thanks;
likewise, south or north, they find some one
skilled in song, generous in gifts,
140 who wishes to exalt his fame before his retinue,
do heroic deeds, till light and life
in ruin fall together: has renown,
gains enduring glory under heaven.

[1] The Myrgings probably came from the region between the Eider and the Elbe. Most of the tribes mentioned in this poem lived on the shores of the North Sea or of the Baltic.

[2] See *Deor* (22), for a reference to Eormanric's 'wolfish' mind. Ealhhild is probably his wife whom he is said to have murdered.

[3] Ætla (or Attila), see *Waldere* (I, 6).

[4] Eormanric sent his son and Becca to woo Swanhild (probably the same as Ealhhild) on his behalf. Becca proved a traitor to both Eormanric and to the son.

[5] Heoden carried off Hagena's daughter Hild.

[6] Wade was the father of Welund. He helped Heoden to carry off Hild. He was credited with power over the sea and with great strength.

[7] The historical king of the sixth century, Theodoric I became a famous figure in later medieval poetry. His son Theodebert conquered Hygelac (see *Beowulf*, sections xix, xxxiii, xxxv, and xl for references to this disastrous expedition).

[8] Apparently the Breca of *Beowulf* (506, 531, 583).

[9] Finn, see *Beowulf* (1068).

[10] Hnæf, see *Beowulf* (1069) and *The Finnsburh Fragment* (2).

[11] Sæferth is the Sigeferth of *The Finnsburh Fragment* (15).

[12] For Ongentheow, see *Beowulf* 2924 ('The Battle of Ravenswood and Death of Ongentheow').

[13] Offa is mentioned in *Beowulf* as the husband of Thryth ('The Tale of Thryth'); here as the champion of the Angles against the Myrgings. Fifeldor is the Eider.

[14] See *Beowulf* 2064 ('The Tale of Freawaru') for Ingeld, son of Froda who married Freawaru, Hrothgar's daughter, after his father was killed in an attack on the Danes. Hrothgar's attempt to make peace by effecting this alliance failed when Ingeld attacked Heorot. The attack was repulsed by Hrothgar and his nephew Hrothulf, though Heorot was burned.

[15] The same Guthhere of *Waldere* (I, 25); historical king of the Burgundians in the fifth century. For centuries he remained a famous figure in poetry. In the *Nibelungenlied* he appears as Gunther.

[16] Ælfwine and his father Eadwine are the Alboin and Audoin (d. 565) of history, kings of the Lombards.

[17] Not the Eadgils of *Beowulf* (2392).

[18] Emerca and Fridla were nephews of Eormanric. East-Gota was an ancestor of Eormanric.

[19] Theodoric the Goth, not Theodoric the Frank mentioned above (24). Seafola was his retainer.

[20] Sifeca was a traitor whose evil advice led Eormanric to put his sons to death.

[21] Hlithe, Incgentheow, and Wyrmhere are probably heroes of the wars between the Huns and Goths.

[22] Withergyld is probably the same as the one mentioned in *Beowulf* (2052). Freotheric is probably the son of Eormanric.

[23] Wudga (or Widia) is a Gothic hero. He is mentioned in *Waldere* (II, 4, 9) as receiving a reward for helping Theodric. Hama is spoken of in *Beowulf* as having robbed Eormanric.

Deor

Deor

Welund[1] him be wurman   wræces cunnade,
anhydig eorl,   earfoþa dreag,
hæfde him to gesiþþe   sorge ond longaþ,
wintercealde wræce;   wean oft onfond,
5   siþþan hine Niðhad[2] on   nede legde,
swoncre seonobende   on syllan monn.
      Þæs ofereode: þisses swa mæg!

Beadohilde[3] ne wæs   hyre broþra deaþ
on sefan swa sar,   swa hyre sylfre þing,
10   þæt heo gearolice   ongieten hæfde
þæt heo eacen wæs;   æfre ne meahte
þriste geþencan,   hu ymb þæt sceolde.
      Þæs ofereode: þisses swa mæg!

We þæt Mæðhilde[4]   monge gefrugnon,
15   wurdon grundlease   Geates[5] frige,
þæt hi seo sorglufu   slæp ealle binom.
      Þæs ofereode: þisses swa mæg!

Ðeodric[6] ahte   þritig wintra
Mæringa burg;   þæt wæs monegum cuþ.
20   Þæs ofereode: þisses swa mæg!

We geascodan   Eormanrices[7]
wylfenne geþoht;   ahte wide folc
Gotena rices.   Þæt wæs grim cyning.
Sæt secg monig   sorgum gebunden,
25   wean on wenan,   wyscte geneahhe,
þæt þæs cynerices   ofercumen wære.
      Þæs ofereode: þisses swa mæg!

Siteð sorcearig,   sælum bidæled,
on sefan sweorceð;   sylfum þinceð,

100

Deor

Welund,[1] entramelled, understood wrack.
He, stubborn *eorl*, suffered privation,
had, as companions, sorrow and longing,
a wintry-cold exile; experienced woes
5   often, once Nithhad[2] laid need upon him,
lithe sinew-bonds on the better man.
　　That passed away; so may this!

Beadohild[3] didn't for her brothers' deaths
feel as sore-stricken as she did for herself,
10   when all too plainly she'd perceived
that she was pregnant; nor ever could she
consider boldly the outcome of that.
　　That passed away; so may this!

Of Mæthhild[4] many of us have heard tell:
15   the Geat's[5] love for her was limitless,
their hapless devotion deprived them of sleep.
　　That passed away; so may this!

For thirty winters Theodric[6] held
the Mærings' stronghold, as many have known.
20   　　That passed away; so may this!

We have heard of Eormanric's[7]
wolfish design; how he widely ruled folk
of the realm of the Goths – a grim king.
Many a man would sit shackled with sorrows,
25   in prospect of woe, and earnestly wish
that his rule were restricted.
　　That passed away; so may this!

The sorrowful one sits deprived of delight,
grows dark in spirit; it seems to him

30   þæt sy endeleas   earfoða dæl.
      Mæg þonne geþencan,   þæt geond þas woruld
      witig Dryhten   wendeþ geneahhe,
      eorle monegum   are gesceawað,
      wislicne blæd,   sumum weana dæl.
35   Þæt ic bi me sylfum   secgan wille,
      þæt ic hwile wæs   Heodeninga[8] scop,
      dryhtne dyre.   Me wæs Deor[9] noma.
      Ahte ic fela wintra   folgað tilne,
      holdne hlaford,   oþþæt Heorrenda[10] nu,
40   leoðcræftig monn   londryht geþah,
      þæt me eorla hleo   ær gesealde.
         Þæs ofereode: þisses swa mæg!

30 that his measure of misery may be without end.
He may then wonder that all through this world
the wise Lord wends constant,
granting grace to many an *eorl*,
certain success, countless sorrows to some.

35 Of myself I will say that I
was once the *scop* of the Heodingas,[8]
dear to my prince. Deor[9] was my name.
For many a winter I had meet office,
a loyal lord, until Heorrenda[10] now,

40 a man skilled in song, received the land-rights
that the refuge of warriors erst rendered me.
That passed away: so may this!

---

[1] Welund, the mythical smith of Germanic legend, Vǫlundr in the *Vǫlundarkviða*, Daedalus or Vulcan in classical mythology. See *Waldere* (I, 2).

[2] Nithhad, or Niðuðr, King of the Niarar, in the *Vǫlundarkviða*.

[3] Beadohild, or Boðvildr, in the *Vǫlundarkviða*, the daughter of Nithhad. Welund slew her two brothers and ravished her to avenge himself on Nithhad. Widia, her son by Welund, is mentioned in *Waldere* (6).

[4] Mæthhild is identified by Kemp Malone (*Deor*, p. 8) with Magnhild, the heroine of a Scandinavian ballad.

[5] Geat, the hero of the ballad afore-mentioned, is there known as Gaute or Gauti.

[6] Theodric, king of the Visigoths, or Mæringas (19).

[7] Eormanric, or Eormanricus, king of the Ostrogoths, flourished in the third quarter of the fourth century A.D.

[8] Heodeningas, a royal family which claimed descent from Heoden whose tribe was the Gloman, according to the poem *Widsith* (21).

[9] Deor, not mentioned elsewhere, probably an invention of the author's, like the minstrel of *Widsith*.

[10] Heorrenda, according to Kemp Malone (*Deor*, p. 37) seems to be the Hjarrandi of Icelandic tradition, whose Danish equivalent, Hjarne, is the minstrel king of Saxo's *Gesta Danorum*.

Wulf and Eadwacer

Wulf and Eadwacer

Leodum is minum   swylce him mon lac gife;
willað hy hine aþecgan,   gif he on þreat cymeð?
    Ungelic is us.
Wulf is on iege,   ic on oþerre.
5   Fæst is þæt eglond,   fenne biworpen.
Sindon wælreowe   weras þær on ige.
Willað hy hine aþecgan,   gif he on þreat cymeð?
    Ungelice is us.
Wulfes ic mines widlastum   wenum dogode;
10 þonne hit wæs renig weder   ond ic reotugu sæt,
þonne mec se beaducafa   bogum bilegde,
wæs me wyn to þon,   wæs me hwæþre eac lað.
Wulf, min Wulf,   wena me þine
seoce gedydon,   þine seldcymas,
15 murnende mod,   nales meteliste.
Gehyrest þu, Eadwacer?   Uncerne earne hwelp
bireð wulf to wuda.
Þæt mon eaþe tosliteð   þætte næfre gesomnad wæs,
uncer giedd geador.

Wulf and Eadwacer

It is to my people as if one gave them a gift;
will they receive him, if he comes as a threat?
  Our lots are different.
Wulf is on one isle, I on another.
5 That isle is a fortress, encircled by fens.
Bloodthirsty men there are on the island.
Will they receive him, if he comes as a threat?
  Our lots are different.
My Wulf's far-wanderings I suffered, hopeful.
10 When the weather was rainy and I weeping sat,
when the brave warrior wound his arms round me,
there was delight in it, yet also disgust.
Wulf, my Wulf, my yearnings for thee
have made me sick, thy seldom coming,
15 my woeful mood, not want of food.
Hearest thou, Eadwacer? Our wretched whelp
Wulf shall carry off to the wood.
One easily sunders what never was joined:
our song together.

Gnomic Verse

Maxims I

A

Frige mec frodum wordum! Ne læt þinne ferð onhælne,
degol þæt þu deopost cunne! Nelle ic þe min dyrne gesecgan,
gif þu me þinne hygecræft hylest ond þine heortan geþohtas.
Gleawe men sceolon gieddum wrixlan. God sceal mon ærest hergan
5 fægre, fæder userne, forþon þe he us æt frymþe geteode
lif ond lænne willan; he usic wile þara leana gemonian.
Meotud sceal in wuldre, mon sceal on eorþan
geong ealdian. God us ece biþ,
ne wendað hine wyrda ne hine wiht dreceþ,
10 adl ne yldo ælmihtigne;
ne gomelað he in gæste, ac he is gen swa he wæs,
þeoden geþyldig. He us geþonc syleð,
missenlicu mod, monge reorde.
Feorhcynna fela fæþmeþ wide
15 eglond monig. Eardas rume
meotud arærde for moncynne,
ælmihtig god, efenfela bega
þeoda ond þeawa. Þing sceal gehegan
frod wiþ frodne; biþ hyra ferð gelic,
20 hi a sace semaþ, sibbe gelærað,
þa ær wonsælge awegen habbað.
Ræd sceal mid snyttro, ryht mid wisum,
til sceal mid tilum. Tu beoð gemæccan;
sceal wif ond wer in woruld cennan
25 bearn mid gebyrdum. Beam sceal on eorðan
leafum liþan, leomu gnornian.
Fus sceal feran, fæge sweltan
ond dogra gehwam ymb gedal sacan
middangeardes. Meotud ana wat
30 hwær se cwealm cymeþ, þe heonan of cyþþe gewiteþ.
Umbor yceð, þa æradl nimeð;
þy weorþeð on foldan swa fela fira cynnes,

Maxims I

A

Ask me with wise words. Let not thy heart be hid,
or the mystery thou mayst know most deeply. I will not tell thee my secret,
if thou concealst from me thy wisdom and thy heart's thoughts.
Sagacious men shall swap speech. One shall first fittingly praise
5   God, our Father, because in the beginning He bestowed on us
life and transitory will. He will remind us of those rewards.
The Maker shall dwell in glory. Men shall live on earth,
the young grow old. God is eternal for us.
Fates change Him not, nor in any way
10 do sickness or age affect Him, the Almighty.
Nor does He grow old in spirit, but He is still as He was,
the patient Prince. He gives us thoughts,
different dispositions, many tongues.
Many an isle in its wide embrace
15 holds many life-species. These broad lands
for mankind the Maker, Almighty God,
created, equally many of both
people and customs. Sage with sage
shall meet. Their minds are similar.
20 They ever settle strife, and counsel peace,
which wretched men have earlier wrecked.
Prudence shall go with wisdom, justice with the wise,
a good man with good men. Two are mates.
Man and wife shall bring into the world
25 children through birth. On earth a tree
shall lose its leaves, lament its limbs.
The dying man shall depart, the doomed man die,
and every day fight against his flight
from the world. God alone knows
30 where the pestilence fares that flies hence from the land.
He increases children, whom early illness takes;
and thus there come to be so many men on earth.

ne sy þæs magutimbres   gemet ofer eorþan,
gif hi ne wanige   se þas woruld teode.
35   Dol biþ se þe his dryhten nat,   to þæs oft cymeð deað unþinged.
Snotre men sawlum beorgað,   healdað hyra soð mid ryhte.
Eadig bið se þe in his eþle geþihð,   earm se him his frynd geswicað.
Nefre sceal se him his nest aspringeð,   nyde sceal þrage gebunden.
Bliþe sceal bealoleas heorte.   Blind sceal his eagna þolian,
40   oftigen biþ him torhtre gesihþe.   Ne magon hi tunglu bewitian,
swegltorht sunnan ne monan;   þæt him biþ sar in his mode,
onge þonne he hit ana wat,   ne weneð þæt him þæs edhwyrft cyme.
Waldend him þæt wite teode,   se him mæg wyrpe syllan,
hælo of heofodgimme,   gif he wat heortan clæne.
45   Lef mon læces behofað.   Læran sceal mon geongne monnan,
trymman ond tyhtan þæt he teala cunne,   oþþæt hine mon atemedne
                                                                                          hæbbe.
Sylle him wist ond wædo,   oþþæt hine mon on gewitte alæde.
Ne sceal hine mon cildgeongne forcweþan,   ær he hine acyþan mote;
þy sceal on þeode geþeon,   þæt he wese þristhycgende.
50   Styran sceal mon strongum mode.   Storm oft holm gebringeþ,
geofen in grimmum sælum;   onginnað grome fundian
fealwe on feorran to londe,   hwæþer he fæste stonde.
Weallas him wiþre healdað,   him biþ wind gemæne.
             Swa biþ sæ smilte,
55   þonne hy wind ne weceð;
swa beoþ þeoda geþwære,   þonne hy geþingad habbað,
gesittað him on gesundum þingum,   ond þonne mid gesiþum healdaþ
cene men gecynde rice.   Cyning biþ anwealdes georn;
lað se þe londes monað,   leof se þe mare beodeð.
60   Þrym sceal mid wlenco,   þriste mid cenum,
sceolun bu recene   beadwe fremman.
Eorl sceal on eos boge,   eorod sceal getrume ridan,
fæste feþa stondan.   Fæmne æt hyre bordan geriseð;
widgongel wif word gespringeð,   oft hy mon wommum bilihð,
65   hæleð hy hospe mænað,   oft hyre hleor abreoþeð.
Sceomiande man sceal in sceade hweorfan,   scir in leohte geriseð.

There would be no limit of progeny on earth
if He who wrought this world did not diminish them.
35   Foolish is he who knows not his Lord, since death often comes
unexpectedly;
wise men save their souls, duly maintain their integrity.
Happy is he who prospers in his home, hapless is he whose friends
are false.
Never shall he be whose store fails, distress shall bind him for a space.
A guiltless heart shall be blithe. A blind man shall suffer the loss of eyes;
40   clear sight is deprived him, nor can he discern the stars,
the radiant sun or moon. That will be grievous to him in his mind,
a sorrow since he alone knows it, and looks not for the return of his sight.
The Lord gave him that punishment; and He can grant a cure,
healing of his head's gem, if He knows his heart is clean.
45   A weak man needs a leech. One shall teach a young man,
encourage and urge him to know well, until one has subdued him.
Let him be given food and clothing till he be brought to understanding.
He shall not be rebuked as a child before he can reveal himself;
he shall then prosper among people because he will be bold and brave.
50   A man shall rule with a strong mind. The sea often brings a storm,
the ocean in fierce weather. Angrily the dun waves start
to hasten from afar off to the land; yet may it hold fast.
The cliffs resist them, they both feel the wind.
        As the sea is serene
55   when the wind wakes it not,
so are tribes tranquil when they come to terms.
They settle in safety, and then amid comrades,
brave men hold a natural sovereignty. A king is eager for power.
Loathed is he who lays claim to land, loved is he who gives more.
60   Power shall go with pride, bold men with brave men;
both shall be prompt to prosecute war.
An *eorl* shall sit on a charger's back, the cavalry ride in company,
the infantry stand fast. It befits a wife to sit at her embroidery;
a gadding woman generates gossip, she often defames herself with vice;
65   men speak of her with contempt; her cheek often fades.
A man who is ashamed shall walk in the shade; a pure man in the light.

Hond sceal heofod inwyrcan, hord in streonum bidan,
gifstol gegierwed stondan, hwonne hine guman gedælen.
Gifre biþ se þam golde onfehð, guma þæs on heahsetle geneah;
70 lean sceal, gif we leogan nellað, þam þe us þas lisse geteode.

Hand shall lie upon head, treasure remain in its resting-place;
the gift-throne stand ready until men share out the hoard.
Greedy is he who receives that gold; the man on the high-seat will
satisfy him.
70 If we will not speak false, we must repay Him who has decreed this
mercy.

B

Forst sceal freosan, fyr wudu meltan,
eorþe growan, is brycgian,
wæter helm wegan, wundrum lucan
eorþan ciþas. An sceal inbindan
5 forstes fetre felameahtig god;
winter sceal geweorpan, weder eft cuman,
sumor swegle hat, sund unstille.
Deop deada wæg dyrne bið lengest;
holen sceal inæled, yrfe gedæled
10 deades monnes. Dom biþ selast.
    Cyning sceal mid ceape cwene gebicgan,
bunum ond beagum; bu sceolon ærest
geofum god wesan. Guð sceal in eorle,
wig geweaxan, ond wif geþeon
15 leof mid hyre leodum, leohtmod wesan,
rune healdan, rumheort beon
mearum ond maþmum, meodorædenne
for gesiðmægen symle æghwær
eodor æþelinga ærest gegretan,
20 forman fulle to frean hond
ricene geræcan, ond him ræd witan
boldagendum bæm ætsomne.
    Scip sceal genægled, scyld gebunden,
leoht linden bord, leof wilcuma
25 Frysan wife, þonne flota stondeð;
biþ his ceol cumen ond hyre ceorl to ham,
agen ætgeofa, ond heo hine in laðaþ,
wæsceð his warig hrægl ond him syleþ wæde niwe,
liþ him on londe þæs his lufu bædeð.
30 Wif sceal wiþ wer wære gehealdan, oft hi mon wommum belihð;
fela bið fæsthydigra, fela bið fyrwetgeornra,
freoð hy fremde monnan, þonne se oþer feor gewiteþ.
Lida biþ longe on siþe; a mon sceal seþeah leofes wenan,
gebidan þæs he gebædan ne mæg. Hwonne him eft gebyre weorðe,

B

Frost shall freeze, fire consume wood,
earth produce growth, ice form a bridge,
water wear helm, wondrously confine
the young sprouts of earth. One shall unbind
5 the fetters of frost, God Almighty.
Winter shall pass, fair weather return,
summer hot with sun. Unquiet the sound.
The deep, dead wave, is longest hid.
Holly shall be kindled, the legacy
10 of a dead man be divided. Glory is best.
     A king shall buy his queen with goods,
with beakers and bracelets. First they must both
be generous with gifts. Warlike valour grown
strong in an *eorl*, the woman shall thrive,
15 loved by the tribe. She shall be cheerful,
keep counsel, and be liberal
with horses and treasures. At the mead-drinking
always everywhere before the band of comrades
she shall greet the protector of *æthelings* first;
20 quickly offer the first cup to the prince's hand
and know wise counsel for the two of them
together in their household.
     The ship shall be nailed, the shield be bound,
the linden targe light. Dear is the loved one
25 to his Frisian wife, when the fleet docks.
His vessel has come, and her man is at home,
her own provider; and she bids him come in,
washes his sea-stained gear, gives him fresh weeds.
grants him on land what his love demands.
30 A wife shall keep faith with her man. Woman is often accused of vice.
Many are constant, many are curious,
loving strange men when the other fares afar.
Long is the sailor away on the voyage, yet one shall ever await a beloved,
await what he cannot hasten for. When he is given the chance,

35 ham cymeð, gif he hal leofað, nefne him holm gestyreð,
    mere hafað mundum mægð egsan wyn.
    Ceap eadig mon cyning wic þonne
    leodon cypeþ, þonne liþan cymeð;
    wuda ond wætres nyttað, þonne him biþ wic alyfed,
40 mete bygeþ, gif he maran þearf, ærþon he to meþe weorþe.
    Seoc se biþ þe to seldan ieteð; þeah hine mon on sunnan læde,
    ne mæg he be þy wedre wesan, þeah hit sy wearm on sumera,
    ofercumen biþ he, ær he acwele, gif he nat hwa hine cwicne fede.
    Mægen mon sceal mid mete fedan, morþor under eorþan befeolan,
45 hinder under hrusan, þe hit forhelan þenceð;
    ne biþ þæt gedefe deaþ, þonne hit gedyrned weorþeð.
       Hean sceal gehnigan, adl gesigan,
    ryht rogian. Ræd biþ nyttost,
    yfel unnyttost, þæt unlæd nimeð.
50 God bið genge, ond wiþ god lenge.
    Hyge sceal gehealden, hond gewealden,
    seo sceal in eagan, snyttro in breostum,
    þær bið þæs monnes modgeþoncas.
    Muþa gehwylc mete þearf, mæl sceolon tidum gongan.
55 Gold geriseþ on guman sweorde,
    sellic sigesceorp, sinc on cwene,
    god scop gumum, garniþ werum,
    wig towiþre wicfreoþa healdan.
    Scyld sceal cempan, sceaft reafere,
60 sceal bryde beag, bec leornere,
    husl halgum men, hæþnum synne.
       Woden worhte weos, wuldor alwalda,
    rume roderas; þæt is rice god,
    sylf soðcyning, sawla nergend,
65 se us eal forgeaf þæt we on lifgaþ,
    ond eft æt þam ende eallum wealdeð
    monna cynne. Þæt is meotud sylfa.

35 he will come home again, if he lives unharmed, unless the sea stays him,
    the ocean has him in its clutches. A maid is the joy of her possessor.
    A wealthy man will sell his goods, and the king quarters
    to a man when he comes sailing in.
    He has use of wood and water when a dwelling is granted him;
40 he buys food, if he need more, ere he grow too faint.
    He who eats too seldom will be ill. Though he be led into the sun,
    he cannot endure the open air; though it be warm in summer,
    he is overcome ere he die, if he knows no one to keep him alive with food.
    Strength shall be nourished with meat; murder be laid underground,
45 down beneath the earth, by him who thinks to hide it.
    That is no seemly death when it is kept secret.
        The humble shall bow down, sickness languish,
    justice flourish. Good counsel is most useful;
    evil most harmful, which the hapless man takes.
50 Good is powerful and pertains to God.
    The mind shall be ruled, the hand controlled;
    sight shall be in the eye, wisdom in the breast
    where man's thoughts are.
    Every mouth craves meat; meals shall come on time.
55 Gold appears seemly on a man's sword,
    rare triumphant raiment, jewels on a woman.
    Men need a good *scop*, heroes fierce fighting
    to hold their homes against attack.
    A warrior shall have a shield, a spoiler a spear;
60 a bride a bracelet, a scholar books,
    a holy man *housel*, a heathen sins.
        Woden wrought idols, the Almighty glory,
    the spacious skies. That is a mighty God,
    the very King of truth, the Saviour of souls.
65 He gave us all that we live by
    and in the end will rule again
    all mankind. He is the Creator Himself.

C

Ræd sceal mon secgan, rune writan,
leoþ gesingan, lofes gearnian,
dom areccan, dæges onettan.
Til mon tiles ond tomes meares,
5 cuþes ond gecostes ond calcrondes;
nænig fira to fela gestryneð.
Wel mon sceal wine healdan on wega gehwylcum;
oft mon fereð feor bi tune, þær him wat freond unwiotodne.
Wineleas, wonsælig mon genimeð him wulfas to geferan,
10 felafæcne deor. Ful oft hine se gefera sliteð;
gryre sceal for greggum, græf deadum men;
hungre heofeð, nales þæt heafe bewindeð,
ne huru wæl wepeð wulf se græga,
morþorcwealm mæcga, ac hit a mare wille.
15 Wræd sceal wunden, wracu heardum men.
Boga sceal stræle, sceal bam gelic
mon to gemæccan. Maþþum oþres weorð,
gold mon sceal gifan. Mæg god syllan
eadgum æhte ond eft niman.
20 Sele sceal stondan, sylf ealdian.
Licgende beam læsest groweð.
Treo sceolon brædan ond treow weaxan,
sio geond bilwitra breost ariseð.
        Wærleas mon ond ungetreow,
25   atrenmod ond ungetreow,
        þæs ne gymeð god.
Fela sceop meotud þæs þe fyrn gewearð, het siþþan swa forð wesan.
Wæra gehwylcum wislicu word gerisað,
gleomen gied ond guman snyttro.
30 Swa monige beoþ men ofer eorþan, swa beoþ modgeþoncas;
        ælc him hafað sundorsefan.
Longað þonne þy læs þe him con leoþa worn,
oþþe mid hondum con hearpan gretan;
hafaþ him his gliwes giefe, þe him god sealde.
35 Earm biþ se þe sceal ana lifgan,

C

A man shall utter wisdom, write runes,
sing songs, earn praise,
expound glory, be diligent daily.
A good man is mindful of a good and tame horse,
5 known, and tried, and round of hoof.
No man will acquire too much.
   On every road one must retain a friend;
often a man avoids a town where he knows he has no certain friend.
Unfriended, unblest, a man makes companions of wolves,
10 very treacherous beasts. Full often that comrade tears him.
There shall be fear of the grey wolf; a grave for the dead man.
It grieves for its hunger, haunts not the grave with dirge,
and certainly the grey wolf weeps not for the slaughter,
the killing of men, but it always wants more.
15 A bandage shall be bound; a rash man have revenge;
The bow shall be for the arrow; and to both alike
shall man be mate. Treasure becomes another's;
a man shall give gold away. God can grant
possessions to the prosperous and take them back again.
20 A hall shall stand, grow old itself.
A fallen tree grows least.
Trees shall spread out and the truth increase;
it springs up in the breast of the simple everywhere.
       A man false and foolish,
25   venomous and faithless –
       God cares not for him.
God shaped much in the beginning, bade them thenceforth so to stay.
For every one wise words are well,
a lay for the gleeman, prudence for the man.
30 There are as many views as men upon earth,
       each has a mind of his own.
He has fewer longings who knows many songs,
or can manage the harp with his hands;
he has his gift of music, which God has granted him.
35 Wretched is he who must live alone,

wineleas wunian hafaþ him wyrd geteod;
betre him wære þæt he broþor ahte, begen hi anes monnes,
eorles eaforan wæran, gif hi sceoldan eofor onginnan
oþþe begen beran; biþ þæt sliþhende deor.
40   A scyle þa rincas gerædan lædan
       ond him ætsomne swefan;
       næfre hy mon tomælde,
       ær hy deað todæle.
    Hy twegen sceolon tæfle ymbsittan, þenden him hyra torn toglide,
45 forgietan þara geocran gesceafta, habban him gomen on borde;
idle hond æmetlan geneah
tæfles monnes, þonne toselum weorpeð.
Seldan in sidum ceole, nefne he under segle yrne,
werig sceal se wiþ winde roweþ; ful oft mon wearnum tihð
50 eargne, þæt he elne forleose, drugað his ar on borde.
    Lot sceal mid lyswe, list mid gedefum;
       þy weorþeð se stan forstolen.
       Oft hy wordum toweorpað,
       ær hy bacum tobreden;
55   geara is hwær aræd.
    Wearð fæhþo fyra cynne, siþþan furþum swealg
eorðe Abeles blode. Næs þæt andæge nið,
of þam wrohtdropan wide gesprungon,
micel mon ældum, monegum þeodum
60 bealoblonden niþ. Slog his broðor swæsne
Cain, þone cwealm nerede; cuþ wæs wide siþþan,
þæt ece nið ældum scod, swa aþolwarum.
Drugon wæpna gewin wide geond eorþan,
ahogodan ond ahyrdon heoro sliþendne.
65   Gearo sceal guþbord, gar on sceafte,
ecg on sweorde ond ord spere,
hyge heardum men. Helm sceal cenum,
ond a þæs heanan hyge hord unginnost.

fate has decreed he shall dwell without friends.
It were better for him that he had a brother, both the same
man's sons, an *eorl*'s, if they should attack a boar,
or both of them a bear – a beast with cruel paws.
40 Ever shall these warriors bear arms
        and sleep together in company;
        never let them through slander be
        divided ere they be parted by death.
    The two shall sit at a game, till their anger slips away,
45 forget the harsh shaping of fate, enjoying sport at the board.
    Idle hands are leisure enough
    for the gamester when he throws the dice,
    but seldom in a broad ship, unless it is running under sail.
    Weary shall he be who runs against the wind. Full often is he reproached
50 with sloth, so he grows disheartened, and draws his oar on board.
    Guile goes with foul play, skill with what is fitting;
        so is a stone stolen.
        Men often bandy words before
        they turn their backs upon each other.
55   The resolute man is everywhere ready.
    Hostility has been with men, even since the earth
    drank Abel's blood. That was no one-day brawl
    from which sprang widely wicked drops,
    much evil for men, for many nations
60 pernicious hate. Cain slew his own brother,
    plotted his killing. Far and wide was it known
    that constant hate did hurt to men. So earth's habitants
    endure the clash of weapons all over the world,
    devising and tempering dangerous swords.
65 The shield shall be ready, the dart on its shaft,
    an edge on the sword, and point on the spear,
    courage in a brave man, helmet for a bold man,
    and ever the least treasure for the coward of soul.

Maxims II

Cyning sceal rice healdan. Ceastra beoð feorran gesyne,
orðanc enta geweorc, þa þe on þysse eorðan syndon,
wrætlic weallstana geweorc. Wind byð on lyfte swiftust,
þunar byð þragum hludast. Þrymmas syndan Cristes myccle,
5 wyrd byð swiðost. Winter byð cealdost,
lencten hrimigost (he byð lengest ceald),
sumor sunwlitegost (swegel byð hatost),
hærfest hreðeadegost, hæleðum bringeð
geres wæstmas, þa þe him god sendeð.
10 Soð bið switolost, sinc byð deorost,
gold gumena gehwam, and gomol snoterost,
fyrngearum frod, se þe ær feala gebideð.
Weax bið wundrum clibbor. Wolcnu scriðað.
Geongne æþeling sceolan gode gesiðas
15 byldan to beaduwe and to beahgife.
Ellen sceal on eorle, ecg sceal wið hellme
hilde gebidan. Hafuc sceal on glofe
wilde gewunian, wulf sceal on bearowe,
earm anhaga, eofor sceal on holte,
20 toðmægenes trum. Til sceal on eðle
domes wyrcean. Daroð sceal on handa,
gar golde fah. Gim sceal on hringe
standan steap and geap. Stream sceal on yðum
mencgan mereflode. Mæst sceal on ceole,
25 segelgyrd seomian. Sweord sceal on bearme,
drihtlic isern. Draca sceal on hlæwe,
frod, frætwum wlanc. Fisc sceal on wætere
cynren cennan. Cyning sceal on healle
beagas dælan. Bera sceal on hæðe,
30 eald and egesfull. Ea of dune sceal
flodgræg feran. Fyrd sceal ætsomne,
tirfæstra getrum. Treow sceal on eorle,
wisdom on were. Wudu sceal on foldan
blædum blowan. Beorh sceal on eorþan

Maxims II

A king shall rule. Cities are conspicuous from afar,
cunning work of giants, which in this world, survive,
wondrous work of wall-stones. Wind is swiftest in the sky,
thunder is loudest in season. Christ's glories are great.
5　*Wyrd* is cruellest, winter coldest,
spring frostiest – for it is longest cold.
Summer sunshine prettiest – the sun is hottest –
harvest most fortunate, as it fetches for men
the year's yield, which God grants them.
10　Truth is most deceptive, treasure is dearest,
as gold is for all men; and an old man is wisest,
sagacious with years, who has erst suffered much.
Woe is wondrous hard to ease. The welkin whirls.
Good comrades must urge a stripling chief
15　to battle and to the bestowal of rings.
A hero must be bold. Edge shall in battle
with helm engage. The hawk on the glove
stay wild. The wolf dwell in the wood,
a wretched recluse; the boar in the brake,
20　secure in strong tusks. A good man shall gain
fame in his land. The dart belongs in the hand,
the spear gaudy with gold. The gem on a ring,
prominent and proud. The stream among waves
mingling with the mere-flood. The mast belongs on a ship,
25　swaying as a sailyard. The sword in the lap,
excellent iron. The dragon shall dwell in a cave,
canny, jealous of jewels. The fish in water
spawn its species. The king in the hall
apportion rings. The bear belongs on the heath,
30　aged and awesome. The river must run
grey down the hill. The *fyrd* hold fast,
a glorious troop. A man be true,
a warrior be wise. The wood on earth
shall bloom and blossom. The hill on the land

35 grene standan.   God sceal on heofenum,
    dæda demend.   Duru sceal on healle,
    rum recedes muð.   Rand sceal on scylde,
    fæst fingra gebeorh.   Fugel uppe sceal
    lacan on lyfte.   Leax sceal on wæle
40 mid sceote scriðan.   Scur sceal on heofenum,
    winde geblanden,   in þas woruld cuman.
    Þeof sceal gangan þystrum wederum.   Þyrs sceal on fenne gewunian
    ana innan lande.   Ides sceal dyrne cræfte,
    fæmne hire freond gesecean,   gif heo nelle on folce geþeon
45 þæt hi man beagum gebicge.   Brim sceal sealte weallan,
    lyfthelm and laguflod   ymb ealra landa gehwylc,
    flowan firgenstreamas.   Feoh sceal on eorðan
    tydran and tynan.   Tungol sceal on heofenum
    beorhte scinan,   swa him bebead meotud.
50 God sceal wið yfele,   geogoð sceal wið yldo,
    lif sceal wið deaþe,   leoht sceal wið þystrum,
    fyrd wið fyrde,   feond wið oðrum,
    lað wið laþe   ymb land sacan,
    synne stælan.   A sceal snotor hycgean
55 ymb þysse worulde gewinn,   wearh hangian,
    fægere ongildan   þæt he ær facen dyde
    manna cynne.   Meotud ana wat
    hwyder seo sawul sceal   syððan hweorfan,
    and ealle þa gastas   þe for gode hweorfað
60 æfter deaðdæge,   domes bidað
    on fæder fæðme.   Is seo forðgesceaft
    digol and dyrne;   drihten ana wat,
    nergende fæder.   Næni eft cymeð
    hider under hrofas,   þe þæt her for soð
65 mannum secge   hwylc sy meotodes gesceaft,
    sigefolca gesetu,   þær he sylfa wunað.

35 stand green. God in the heavens,
    Judge of deeds. The door in the hall,
    the building's wide mouth. The boss on the shield,
    a firm finger-guard. The bird shall sport
    aloft in the sky. The salmon in the pool
40 dart with the trout. The shower in the skies,
    mingled with wind, descend on this world.
    A felon go forth in murky weather. A demon dwell in the fen,
    alone in his realm. With secret craft a girl,
    a woman, must seek her friend, if she will not have her folk
45 buy her with rings. The sea must surge with salt;
    cloud-cover and ocean-flood, round every land,
    mountain streams must flow. Cattle on the earth
    breed and teem. The star in the skies
    shine bright as the Ruler bade.
50 Good must strive with evil, youth with age,
    life with death, light with darkness,
    fyrd with *fyrd*, foes with one another,
    round about the land meet force with force,
    avenge hostility. The wise man shall ever think
55 of conflicts in this world. The criminal must hang,
    atone for the crime he committed once
    against mankind. The Lord alone knows
    whither that soul shall afterwards pass,
    and all those spirits who go before God
60 after their death-day. They abide their doom
    in the Father's embrace. One's future fate
    is dark and undisclosed; the Lord alone knows,
    the Father who redeems. No man returns
    here under our roofs who truly may
65 reveal to men the Ruler's mould,
    the victors' homes, where He Himself abides.

127

Charms

1. For Unfruitful Land

Her ys seo bot, hu ðu meaht þine æceras betan gif hi nellaþ wel wexan oþþe þær hwilc ungedefe þing on gedon bið on dry oððe on lyblace. Genim þonne on niht, ær hyt dagige, feower tyrf on feower healfa þæs landes, and gemearca hu hy ær stodon. Nim þonne ele and hunig and beorman, and ælces feos meolc þe on þæm lande sy, and ælces treowcynnes dæl þe on þæm lande sy gewexen, butan heardan beaman, and ælcre namcuþre wyrte dæl, butan glappan anon, and do þonne haligwæter ðær on, and drype þonne þriwa on þone staðol þara turfa, and cweþe ðonne ðas word: Crescite, wexe, et multiplicamini, and gemænigfealda, et replete, and gefylle, terre, þas eorðan. In nomine patris et filii et spiritus sancti sit benedicti.[1] And Pater noster swa oft swa þæt oðer. And bere siþþan ða turf to ciricean, and mæssepreost asinge feower mæssan ofer þan turfon, and wende man þæt grene to ðan weofode, and siþþan gebringe man þa turf þær hi ær wæron ær sunnan setlgange. And hæbbe him gæworht of cwicbeame feower Cristes mælo and awrite on ælcon ende: Matheus and Marcus, Lucas and Iohannes. Lege þæt Cristes mæl on þone pyt neoþeweardne, cweðe ðonne: Crux Matheus, crux Marcus, crux Lucas, crux sanctus Iohannes. Nim ðonne þa turf and sete ðær ufon on and cweþe ðonne nigon siþon þas word, Crescite, and swa oft Pater noster, and wende þe þonne eastweard, and onlut nigon siðon eadmodlice, and cweð þonne þas word:

Eastweard ic stande,   arena ic me bidde,
bidde ic þone mæran domine,   bidde ðone miclan drihten,
bidde ic ðone haligan   heofonrices weard,
eorðan ic bidde   and upheofon
5   and ða soþan   sancta Marian
and heofones meaht   and heahreced,
þæt ic mote þis gealdor   mid gife drihtnes
toðum ontynan   þurh trumne geþanc,
aweccan þas wæstmas   us to woruldnytte,
10   gefyllan þas foldan   mid fæste geleafan,
wlitigigan þas wancgturf,   swa se witega cwæð
þæt se hæfde are on eorþrice,   se þe ælmyssan
dælde domlice   drihtnes þances.

1. For Unfruitful Land

Here is the remedy, by which thou canst improve thy fields if they will not produce well or if any harm has been done to them by sorcery or witchcraft. Take then at night, ere dawn, four sods from four sides of the land and mark how they stood before. Then take oil and honey and yeast, and milk of all the cattle that are on the land, and part of every kind of tree that grows on the land, except hard trees, and part of every well-known herb, except burdock only, and pour holy water thereon, and then let it drop three times on the bottom of the sods, and say then these words: '*Crescite*, (grow,) *et multiplicamini*, (and multiply,) *et replete*, (and fill,) *terre*. (the earth.) *In nomine patris et filii et spiritus sancti sitis benedicti*.'[1] And Paternoster as often as the other. And afterwards carry the sods to church and have a masspriest sing four masses over the sods, and let the green sides be turned to the altar, and later let the sods be brought ere sunset to where they stood before. And let him have four crosses wrought of aspen wood and write on each end *Mattheus* and *Marcus*, *Lucas* and *Johannes*. Lay the cross at the bottom of the pit. Say then: *Crux Matheus, crux Marcus, crux Lucas, crux Sanctus Johannes*. Then take the sods and place them thereon, and then say nine times these words: '*Crescite ...*,' and as often Paternoster, and then turn to the east and bow humbly nine times, and then say these words:

> Eastward I stand, for favours I pray,
> I pray the great Lord, pray the mighty prince,
> I pray the holy Protector of heaven,
> earth I pray and sky
> 5   and the truly holy Mary
> and heaven's might and high hall,
> that by the grace of God this charm
> I may pronounce; by strong resolve
> raise these crops for our worldly use;
> 10 by firm faith fill these fields,
> make beautiful these meadows; as the prophet said
> that he found favour here on earth who gave
> alms wisely, in accordance with God's will.

Wende þe þonne III sunganges, astrece þonne on andlang and arim
þær letanias and cweð þonne: Sanctus, sanctus, sanctus oþ ende.
Sing þonne Benedicite aþenedon earmon and Magnificat and Pater
noster III, and bebeod hit Criste and sancta Marian and þære halgan
rode to lofe and to weorþinga and to are þam þe þæt land age and
eallon þam þe him underðeodde synt. Ðonne þæt eall sie gedon,
þonne nime man uncuþ sæd æt ælmesmannum and selle him twa
swylc, swylce man æt him nime, and gegaderie ealle his sulhgeteogo
togædere; borige þonne on þam beame stor and finol and gehalgode
sapan and gehalgod sealt. Nim þonne þæt sæd, sete on þæs sules
bodig, cweð þonne:

Erce, Erce, Erce,   eorþan modor,
15   geunne þe se alwalda,   ece drihten,
æcera wexendra   and wridendra,
eacniendra   and elniendra,
sceafta hehra,   scirra wæstma,
and þæra bradan   berewæstma,
20   and þæra hwitan   hwætewæstma,
and ealra   eorþan wæstma.
Geunne him   ece drihten
and his halige,   þe on heofonum synt,
þæt hys yrþ si gefriþod   wið ealra feonda gehwæne,
25   and heo si geborgen   wið ealra bealwa gehwylc,
þara lyblaca   geond land sawen.
Nu ic bidde ðone waldend,   se ðe ðas woruld gesceop,
þæt ne sy nan to þæs cwidol wif   ne to þæs cræftig man
þæt awendan ne mæge   word þus gecwedene.

Þonne man þa sulh forð drife and þa forman furh onsceote, cweð
þonne:

30   Hal wes þu, folde,   fira modor!
Beo þu growende   on godes fæþme,
fodre gefylled   firum to nytte.

Nim þonne ælces cynnes melo and abacæ man innewerdre handa
bradnæ hlaf and gecned hine mid meolce and mid haligwætere and
lecge under þa forman furh. Cweþe þonne:

Then turn three times with the course of the sun, then stretch thyself
flat and recite the litanies there; and then say, *Sanctus sanctus,
sanctus*, to the end. Then sing *Benedicite* with arms outstretched and
Magnificat and Paternoster three times, and commend it to the praise
of Christ and holy Mary and the sacred Rood and to the benefit of
him who owns the land and of all those who are subject to him. When
all that is done, then let unknown seed be taken from beggars and let
them be given twice as much as is taken from them. And let him
gather all his ploughing implements together; then bore the plough-
tail and put in incense and fennel and hallowed soap and hallowed
salt. Then take the seed, place it on the body of the plough, then say:

> Erce, Erce, Erce, mother of earth,
> may the Almighty, eternal Lord, grant thee
> fields growing and thriving,
> fruitful and reviving,
> bright shafts of millet-crops,
> and broad barley-crops,
> and white wheat-crops,
> and all the crops of the earth.
> May the eternal Lord grant him,
> and his saints, who are in heaven,
> that his land be kept safe from every foe,
> and it be secure against every harm
> from witchcrafts sown throughout the land.
> Now I pray the Ruler who wrought this world
> that no witch so eloquent, nor man so potent,
> there be to pervert the words thus pronounced.

Then let the plough be driven forth and the first furrow cut. Then say:

> Hail to thee, earth, mother of men!
> Be thou fruitful in God's embrace,
> filled with food for the use of men.

Then take flour of every kind and let a loaf be baked as broad as the
inside of the hands, and knead it with milk and with holy water, and
lay it under the first furrow. Say then:

133

Ful æcer fodres   fira cinne,
beorhtblowende,   þu gebletsod weorþ
35   þæs haligan noman   þe ðas heofon gesceop
and ðas eorþan   þe we on lifiaþ;
se god, se þas grundas geworhte,   geunne us growende gife,
þæt us corna gehwylc   cume to nytte.

Cweð þonne III Crescite in nomine patris, sit benedicti.[2] Amen and
Pater noster þriwa.

Field full of food for the race of men
brightly blooming, be thou blessed
35 in the holy name of Him who shaped this heaven
and this earth on which we live.
May the God who wrought these lands grant us
growing gifts that prove each grain of use.

Then say three times '*Crescite, in nomine patris, sitis benedicti.*'[2]
Amen and Paternoster three times.

---

[1] In the name of the Father and the Son and of the Holy Spirit may you be
blessed.

[2] Grow, in the name of the Father, may you be blessed.

2. The Nine Herbs Charm

Gemyne ðu, mucgwyrt,   hwæt þu ameldodest,
hwæt þu renadest   æt Regenmelde.
Una þu hattest,   yldost wyrta.
Ðu miht wið III   and wið XXX,
þu miht wiþ attre   and wið onflyge,
þu miht wiþ þam laþan   ðe geond lond færð.
Ond þu, wegbrade,   wyrta modor,
eastan openo,   innan mihtigu;
ofer ðe crætu curran,   ofer ðe cwene reodan,
ofer ðe bryde bryodedon,   ofer þe fearras fnærdon.
Eallum þu þon wiðstode   and wiðstunedest;
swa ðu wiðstonde   attre and onflyge
and þæm laðan   þe geond lond fereð.
Stune hætte þeos wyrt,   heo on stane geweox;
stond heo wið attre,   stunað heo wærce.
Stiðe heo hatte,   wiðstunað heo attre,
wreceð heo wraðan,   weorpeð ut attor.
Þis is seo wyrt   seo wiþ wyrm gefeaht,
þeos mæg wið attre,   heo mæg wið onflyge,
heo mæg wið ðam laþan   ðe geond lond fereþ.
Fleoh þu nu, attorlaðe,   seo læsse ða maran,
seo mare þa læssan,   oððæt him beigra bot sy.
Gemyne þu, mægðe,   hwæt þu ameldodest,
hwæt ðu geændadest   æt Alorforda;
þæt næfre for gefloge   feorh ne gesealde
syþðan him mon mægðan   to mete gegyrede.
Þis is seo wyrt   ðe wergulu hatte;
ðas onsænde seolh   ofer sæs hrygc
ondan attres   oþres to bote.
Ðas VIIII magon   wið nygon attrum.
Wyrm com snican,   toslat he man;
ða genam Woden   VIIII wuldortanas,
sloh ða þa næddran,   þæt heo on VIIII tofleah.
Þær geændade   æppel and attor,
þæt heo næfre ne wolde   on hus bugan.

2. The Nine Herbs Charm

Remember, Mugwort, what thou didst reveal,
what thou didst arrange at Regenmeld.
Thou wert called Una, the oldest of herbs,
thou power against three and against thirty,
5   thou power against poison and against infection,
thou power against the foe who fares through the land.
And thou, Plantain, mother of herbs,
open from the east, mighty within;
over thee chariots creaked, over thee queens rode,
10   over thee brides made outcry, over thee bulls gnashed their teeth.
All these thou didst withstand and resist;
so mayst thou withstand poison and infection,
and the foe who fares through the land.
This herb is called Stune; it grew on a stone,
15   it withstands poison, it resists pain.
It is called harsh, it fights against poison,
drives out the hostile one, casts out poison.
This is the herb that fought with the worm;
this power against poison, this power against infection,
20   the power against the foe who fares through the land.
Now, cock's-spur grass, conquer the greater poisons, though thou
art the lesser,
thou, the mightier, conquer the lesser until he be rid of both.
Remember thou, Camomile, what thou didst make known,
what thou didst accomplish at Alorford;
25   that he never yielded his life for infection,
after Camomile was served up as food.
This is the herb which is called Wergulu;
the seal sent this over the back of the sea,
to heal the harm of other venoms.
30   These nine have power against nine poisons.
A worm came crawling, it bit a man.
Then Woden took nine glory-twigs,
smote the adder so that it split into nine.
There ended Apple and poison
35   that she nevermore would enter her house.

Fille and finule, felamihtigu twa,
þa wyrte gesceop witig drihten,
halig on heofonum, þa he hongode;
sette and sænde on VII worulde
40 earmum and eadigum eallum to bote.
Stond heo wið wærce, stunað heo wið attre,
seo mæg wið III and wið XXX,
wið feondes hond and wið færbregde,
wið malscrunge manra wihta.
45 Nu magon þas VIIII wyrta wið nygon wuldorgeflogenum,
wið VIIII attrum and wið nygon onflygnum,
wið ðy readan attre, wið ðy runlan attre,
wið ðy hwitan attre, wið ðy wedenan attre,
wið ðy geolwan attre, wið ðy grenan attre,
50 wið ðy wonnan attre, wið ðy wedenan attre,
wið ðy brunan attre, wið ðy basewan attre,
wið wyrmgeblæd, wið wætergeblæd,
wið þorngeblæd, wið þstelgeblæd,
wið ysgeblæd, wið attorgeblæd,
55 gif ænig attor cume eastan fleogan
oððe ænig norðan * * * cume
oððe ænig westan ofer werðeode.
Crist stod ofer adle ængan cundes.
Ic ana wat ea rinnende
60 þær þa nygon nædran nean behealdað;
motan ealle weoda nu wyrtum aspringan,
sæs toslupan, eal sealt wæter,
ðonne ic þis attor of ðe geblawe.

Mugcwyrt, wegbrade þe eastan open sy, lombescyrse, attorlaðan,
mægeðan, netelan, wudusuræppel, fille and finul, ealde sapan.
Gewyrc ða wyrta to duste, mængc wiþ þa sapan and wið þæs æpples
gor. Wyrc slypan of wætere and of axsan, genim finol, wyl on þære
slyppan and beþe mid æggemongc, þonne he þa sealfe on do, ge ær ge
æfter. Sing þæt galdor on ælcre þara wyrta, III ær he hy wyrce and on
þone æppel ealswa; ond singe þon men in þone muð and in þa earan
buta and on ða wunde þæt ilce gealdor, ær he þa sealfe on do.

Chervil and fennel, the fearsome two,
these herbs the wise Lord, holy in heaven,
wrought while He hung (on the cross);
placed and put in seven worlds
40   poor and rich as an aid to all.
It stands against pain, stands against poison,
it has power against three and against thirty,
against a fiend's hand and against sudden trick,
against the witchcraft of evil wights.
45   Now these nine herbs have power against nine evil spirits,
against nine poisons and against nine infections:
against the red poison, against the running poison,
against the white poison, against the purple poison,
against the yellow poison, against the green poison,
50   against the black poison, against the blue poison,
against the brown poison, against the crimson poison;
against worm-blister, against water-blister,
against thorn-blister, against thistle-blister,
against ice-blister, against poison-blister.
55   If any poison comes flying from the east,
or any from the north, (or any from the south),
or any from the west upon the people.
    Christ stood over disease of every kind.
I alone know running water
60   where the nine adders look upon it close.
May all the weeds now spring up herbs,
seas dissolve, all salty water,
when I blow this poison from thee.

Mugwort, plantain which is open from the east, lamb's cress, cock's-spur grass, camomile, nettle, crab-apple, chervil and fennel, old soap. Pound the herbs to a powder, mix them with the soap and with the juice of the apple. Prepare a paste of water and of ashes; take fennel, boil it in the paste and bathe with a beaten egg, when he applies the salve, both before and after. Sing this charm on each of the herbs, three times before he prepare them and on the apple likewise; and sing the same charm into the mouth and into both the ears of the man and upon the wound, before he applies the salve.

3. Against a Dwarf

Wið dweorh man sceal niman VII lytle oflætan, swylce man mid ofrað, and writan þas naman on ælcre oflætan: Maximianus, Malchus, Iohannes, Martimianus, Dionisius, Constantinus, Serafion. Þænne eft þæt galdor, þæt her æfter cweð, man sceal singan, ærest on þæt wynstre eare, þænne on þæt swiðre eare, þænne bufan þæs mannes moldan. And ga þænne an mædenman to and ho hit on his sweoran, and do man swa þry dagas; him bið sona sel.

Her com in gangan,   in spiderwiht,
hæfde him his haman on handa,   cwæð þæt þu his hæncgest wære,
legde þe his teage an sweoran.   Ongunnan him of þæm lande liþan;
sona swa hy of þæm lande coman,   þa ongunnan him ða liþu colian.
5   Þa com in gangan   dweores sweostar;
þa geændade heo   and aðas swor
ðæt næfre þis ðæm adlegan   derian ne moste,
ne þæm þe þis galdor   begytan mihte,
oððe þe þis galdor   ongalan cuþe. Amen. Fiað.[1]

3. Against a Dwarf

One must take seven little wafers, such as one uses in worship, and write these names on each wafer: *Maximianus, Malchus, Johannes, Martimianus, Dionisius, Constantinus, Serafion.* Then one must sing the charm that is mentioned hereafter, first into the left ear, then into the right ear, then over the man's head. And then let a maiden go to him and hang it upon his neck, and do so for three days; he will soon be better.

> Here a spider-wight came stalking in.
> He had his dress in his hand. He said that thou wert his steed,
> he laid his bonds on thy neck. They began to sail from the land.
> As soon as they left the land, then his limbs began to cool.
> 5   Then the dwarf's sister came stalking in.
> Then she made an end and swore oaths
> that this should never hurt the sick,
> nor him who could obtain this charm,
> nor him who knew to chant this charm. Amen. *Fiat.*[1]

---

[1] Let it be done.

4. For a Sudden Stitch

Wið færstice feferfuige and seo reade netele, ðe þurh ærn inwyxð, and wegbrade; wyll in buteran.

Hlude wæran hy, la, hlude,   ða hy ofer þone hlæw ridan,
wæran anmode,   ða hy ofer land ridan.
Scyld ðu ðe nu,   þu ðysne nið genesan mote.
Ut, lytel spere,   gif her inne sie!
5   Stod under linde,   under leohtum scylde,
þær ða mihtigan wif   hyra mægen beræddon
and hy gyllende   garas sændan;
ic him oðerne   eft wille sændan,
fleogende flane   forane togeanes.
10   Ut, lytel spere,   gif hit her inne sy!
Sæt smið,   sloh seax lytel,
* * * iserna,   wundrum swiðe.
Ut, lytel spere,   gif her inne sy!
Syx smiðas sætan,   wælspera worhtan.
15   Ut, spere,   næs in, spere!
Gif her inne sy   isernes dæl,
hægtessan geweorc,   hit sceal gemyltan.
Gif ðu wære on fell scoten   oððe hit wære on flæsc scoten
oððe wære on blod scoten
20   oððe wære on lið scoten,   næfre ne sy ðin lif atæsed;
gif hit wære esa gescot   oððe hit wære ylfa gescot
oððe hit wære hægtessan gescot,   nu ic wille ðin helpan.
Þis ðe to bote esa gescotes,   ðis ðe to bote ylfa gescotes,
ðis ðe to bote hægtessan gescotes;   ic ðin wille helpan.
25   Fleoh þær * * * on fyrgenheafde.
Hal westu,   helpe ðin drihten!

Nim þonne þæt seax, ado on wætan.

4. For a Sudden Stitch

Feverfew and the red nettle that grows through a house and plantain;
boil in butter.

Loud were they, lo! loud, when they rode over the hill,
fierce were they when they rode over the land.
Shield thyself now, that thou mayst survive this violence.
Out little spear, if herein thou be!
5   I stood under linden-wood, under a light shield,
where the mighty women gathered their strength,
and sent their screaming spears forth;
I will send them back another
arrow flying in their faces.
10   Out little spear, if herein thou be!
A smith sat, forged a little knife,
..... sore smitten with iron.
Out little spear, if herein thou be!
Six smiths sat, wrought war-spears.
15   Out spear, not in, spear!
If herein be aught of iron,
work of witches, it shall melt.
If thou wert shot in the skin, or wert shot in the flesh,
or wert shot in the blood, (or wert shot in the bone),
20   or wert shot in a limb, may thy life never be armed;
If it were the shot of Æsir, or if it were the shot of elves,
or it were the shot of hags, I will help thee now.
This to cure thee of the shot of Æsir, this to cure thee of the shot of
                                                                    elves,
this to cure thee of the shot of hags; I will help thee.
25   Flee to the mountain-head.
Be thou whole. May the Lord help thee.

Take then the knife; plunge it into the liquid.

5. For Loss of Cattle

Þonne þe mon ærest secge þæt þin ceap sy losod, þonne cweð þu ærest, ær þu elles hwæt cweþe:

Bæðleem hatte seo buruh þe Crist on acænned wæs,
seo is gemærsod geond ealne middangeard;
swa þyos dæd for monnum mære gewurþe

þurh þa haligan Cristes rode! Amen. Gebide þe þonne þriwa east and cweþ þonne þriwa: Crux Christi ab oriente reducað.[1] Gebide þe þonne þriwa west and cweð þonne þriwa: Crux Christi ab occidente reducat.[2] Gebide þe þonne þriwa suð and cweþ þriwa: Crux Christi ab austro reducat.[3] Gebide þonne þriwa norð and cweð þriwa: Crux Christi ab aquilone reducað, crux Christi abscondita est et inuenta est.[4] Iudeas Crist ahengon, dydon dæda þa wyrrestan, hælon þæt hy forhelan ne mihtan. Swa þeos dæd nænige þinga forholen ne wurþe þurh þa haligan Cristes rode. Amen.

5. For Loss of Cattle

As soon as someone tells thee that thy goods are lost, then thou must say first of all, before thou sayst anything else:

As the town called Bethlehem where Christ was born
is well known the whole world over,
so may this deed be known among men,

through the holy cross of Christ! Amen. Then worship three times towards the east and say three times: '*Crux Christi ab oriente reducath.*'[1] Then worship three times towards the west and say three times: '*Crux Christi ab occidente reducat.*'[2] Then worship three times towards the south and say three times: '*Crux Christi ab austro reducat.*'[3] Then worship three times towards the north and say three times: '*Crux Christi ab aquilone reducath, crux abscondita est et inuenta est.*'[4] The Jews hanged Christ, treated Him most evilly, concealed what they could not keep hidden. So may this deed be concealed in no way, through Christ's holy cross. Amen.

---

[1] Let the cross of Christ bring [it] back from the east.
[2] Let the cross of Christ bring [it] back from the west.
[3] Let the cross of Christ bring [it] back from the south.
[4] Let the cross of Christ bring [it] back from the north, the cross has been hidden and is found.

6. For Delayed Birth

Se wifman, se hire cild afedan ne mæg, gange to gewitenes mannes birgenne and stæppe þonne þriwa ofer þaa byrgenne and cweþe þonne þriwa þas word:

> Þis me to bote   þære laþan lætbyrde,
> þis me to bote   þære swæran swærbyrde,
> þis me to bote   þære laðan lambyrde.

And þonne þæt wif seo mid bearne and heo to hyre hlaforde on reste ga, þonne cweþe heo:

> Up ic gonge,   ofer þe stæppe
5 > mid cwican cilde,   nalæs mid cwellendum,
> mid fulborenum,   nalæs mid fægan.

And þonne seo modor gefele þæt þæt bearn si cwic, ga þonne to cyrican, and þonne heo toforan þan weofode cume, cweþe þonne:

> Criste, ic sæde,   þis gecyþed!

Se wifmon, se hyre bearn afedan ne mæge, genime heo sylf hyre agenes cildes gebyrgenne dæl, wry æfter þonne on blace wulle and bebicge to cepemannum and cweþe þonne:

> Ic hit bebicge,   ge hit bebicgan,
> þas sweartan wulle   and þysse sorge corn.

Se wifman, se ne mæge bearn afedan, nime þonne anes bleos cu meoluc on hyre handæ and gesupe þonne mid hyre muþe and gange þonne to yrnendum wætere and spiwe þær in þa meolc and hlade þonne mid þære ylcan hand þæs wæteres muð fulne and forswelge. Cweþe þonne þas word:

10 > Gehwer ferde ic me þone mæran   maga þihtan,
> mid þysse mæran   mete þihtan;
> þonne ic me wille habban   and ham gan.

Þonne heo to þan broce ga, þonne ne beseo heo, no ne eft þonne heo þanan ga, and þonne ga heo in oþer hus oþer heo ut ofeode and þær gebyrge metes.

6. For Delayed Birth

The woman, who cannot bring her child to maturity, must go to a dead man's grave, step three times over the grave and say these words three times:

> This as my help against the evil late birth,
> this as my help against the grievous dismal birth,
> this as my help against the evil lame birth.

And when that woman is with child and she goes to bed to her lord, then she must say:

> Up I go, I step over thee
> 5   with a live child, not with a dying one,
> with a full-born child, not with a doomed one.

And when the mother feels that the child is alive, she must go to church, and when she comes in front of the altar, then she must say:

> Christ, I said, made this known!

The woman who cannot bring her child to maturity must take part of the grave of her own child, wrap it up in black wool and sell it to merchants. And then she must say:

> I sell it, ye must sell it,
> this black wool and the seeds of this grief.

The woman who cannot bring her child to maturity must take the milk of a cow of one colour in her hand, sip up a little with her mouth, and then go to running water and spit the milk into it. And then with the same hand she must take a mouthful of water and swallow it. Let her then say these words:

> 10   I carried this great strong one with me everywhere,
> strong because of this great food;
> such a one I want to have and go home with.

When she goes to the stream she must not look round, nor again when she goes away from there, and let her go into a house other than the one from which she started, and there take food.

7. For the Water-elf Disease

Gif mon biþ on wæterælfadle, þonne beoþ him þa handnæglas wonne
and þa eagan tearige and wile locian niþer. Do him þis to læcedome:
eoforþrote, cassuc, fone nioþoweard, eowberge, elehtre, eolone,
merscmealwan crop, fenminte, dile, lilie, attorlaþe, polleie, marubie,
docce, ellen, felterre, wermod, streawbergean leaf, consolde; ofgeot
mid ealaþ, do hæligwæter to, sing þis gealdor ofer þriwa:

Ic benne awrat   betst beadowræda,
swa benne ne burnon,   ne burston,
ne fundian,   ne feologan,
ne hoppettan,   ne wund waxsian,
5   ne dolh diopian;   ac him selfe healde halewæge,
ne ace þe þon ma,   þe eorþan on eare ace.

Sing þis manegum siþum: Eorþe þe onbere eallum hire mihtum and
mægenum. Þas galdor mon mæg singan on wunde.

148

7. For the Water-elf Disease

If anyone has the water-elf disease, then his fingernails will be pale and his eyes watery and he will want to look down. Apply this as a medicine for him: Carline thistle, hassock, the nether part of iris, yew-berry, lupine, elecampane, marshmallow head, fen-mint, dill, lily, cock's-spur grass, pennyroyal, horehound, dock, elder, earthgall, wormwood, strawberry leaves, comfrey; soak in ale, add holy water, sing this charm three times:

> I have bound the wounds with the best of war-bands,
> that the wounds neither burn nor burst,
> nor spread, nor go bad,
> nor throb; nor the injuries increase,
> nor the sores deepen; but the health-cup holds it,
> nor will it ache thee more than earth aches in thy ear.

5

Sing this many times: May the earth destroy thee with all her might and main. These charms can be sung on a wound.

8. For a Swarm of Bees

Wið ymbe nim eorþan, oferweorp mid þinre swiþran handa under þinum swiþran fet, and cwet:

Fo ic under fot,   funde ic hit.
Hwæt, eorðe mæg   wið ealra wihta gehwilce
and wið andan   and wið æminde
and wið þa micelan   mannes tungan.

And wiððon forweorp ofer greot, þonne hi swirman, and cweð:

5   Sitte ge, sigewif,   sigað to eorþan!
Næfre ge wilde   to wuda fleogan.
Beo ge swa gemindige   mines godes,
swa bið manna gehwilc   metes and eþeles.

8. For a Swarm of Bees

Take earth, sprinkle it with thy right hand under thy right foot and say:

I hold it under foot; I have found it.
Lo, earth can prevail against every wight,
and against malice, and against mindlessness,
and against the mighty tongue of man.

And then cast gravel over them, when they swarm, and say:

5   Stay, victorious women, sink to earth!
Never fly wild to the wood.
Be as mindful of my good
as each man is of food and home.

9. For Theft of Cattle

Ne forstolen ne forholen nanuht, þæs ðe ic age, þe ma ðe mihte Herod urne drihten. Ic geþohte sancte Eadelenan and ic geþohte Crist on rode ahangen; swa ic þence þis feoh to findanne, næs to oðfeorrganne, and to witanne, næs to oðwyrceanne, and to lufianne, næs to oðlædanne.

Garmund,   godes ðegen,
find þæt feoh   and fere þæt feoh
and hafa þæt feoh   and heald þæt feoh
and fere ham þæt feoh.

5   Þæt he næfre næbbe landes,   þæt he hit oðlæde,
ne foldan,   þæt hit oðferie,
ne husa,   þæt he hit oðhealde.
Gif hyt hwa gedo,   ne gedige hit him næfre!
Binnan þrym nihtum   cunne ic his mihta,

10 his mægen and his mihta   and his mundcræftas.
Eall he weornige,   swa syre wudu weornie,
swa breðel seo swa þystel,
se ðe ðis feoh   oðfergean þence
oððe ðis orf   oðehtian ðence. Amen.

9. For Theft of Cattle

May naught that I own be stolen or concealed, any more than Herod could do to our Lord. I thought of St Helena, and I thought of Christ hanging on the cross; so I look to finding these cattle, not to having them carried away, and to knowing of them, not to losing them, and to having them cared for, not being led away.

Garmund, servant of God,
find those cattle and fetch those cattle,
and have those cattle and hold those cattle,
and carry those cattle home.
5   That he may never have land to lead them to,
nor ground to carry them to,
nor houses to hold them in.
If any do so, may he never thrive by it.
Within three nights I shall know his powers,
10   his main and his might and his skill to protect.
May he wholly wither, as fire withers wood,
be as fragile as a thistle,
he who thinks to steal these cattle,
or thinks to carry off these kine. Amen.

10. For Loss of Cattle

Ðis man sceal cweðan ðonne his ceapa hwilcne man forstolenne. Cwyð ær he ænyg oþer word cweðe:

Bethlem hattæ seo burh ðe Crist on geboren wes,
seo is gemærsod ofer ealne middangeard;
swa ðeos dæd wyrþe for monnum mære,

per crucem Christi! And gebide þe ðonne þriwa east and cweð þriwa: Crux Christi ab oriente reducat. And III west and cweð: Crux Christi ab occidente reducat. And III suð and cweð: Crux Christi a meridie reducant. And III norð and cweð: Crux Christi abscondita sunt et inuenta est. Iudeas Crist ahengon, gedidon him dæda þa wyrstan; hælon þæt hi forhelan ne mihton. Swa næfre ðeos dæd forholen ne wyrðe per crucem Christi.

10. For Loss of Cattle

This must be sung by the man who has been robbed of some of his goods. He must say before he speaks any other word:

Bethlehem is the name of the town where Christ was born.
It is well known throughout the whole world.
So may this act become known among men.

By the cross of Christ! And worship three times to the east and say three times: The cross of Christ will bring it back from the east. And towards the west and say: The cross of Christ will bring it back from the west. And towards the south and say three times: The cross of Christ will bring it back from the south. And towards the north and say: The cross of Christ was hidden and it is found. The Jews hanged Christ, they treated Him in a most evil way. So may this deed never be concealed. By the cross of Christ.

11. A Journey Charm

Ic me on þisse gyrde beluce   and on godes helde bebeode
wið þane sara stice,   wið þane sara slege,
wið þane grymma gryre,
wið ðane micela egsa   þe bið eghwam lað,
5   and wið eal þæt lað   þe in to land fare.
Sygegealdor ic begale,   sigegyrd ic me wege,
wordsige and worcsige.   Se me dege;
ne me mere ne gemyrre,   ne me maga ne geswence,
ne me næfre minum feore   forht ne gewurþe,
10   ac gehæle me ælmihtig and sunu   and frofre gast,
ealles wuldres   wyrðig dryhten,
swa swa ic gehyrde   heofna scyppende.
Abrame and Isace
and swilce men,   Moyses and Iacob,
15   and Dauit and Iosep
and Evan and Annan   and Elizabet,
Saharie and ec Marie,   modur Cristes,
and eac þæ gebroþru,   Petrus and Paulus,
and eac þusend   þinra engla
20   clipige ic me to are   wið eallum feondum.
Hi me ferion and friþion   and mine fore nerion,
eal me gehealdon,   me gewealdon,
worces stirende;   si me wuldres hyht,
hand ofer heafod,   haligra rof,
25   sigerofra sceolu,   soðfæstra engla.
Biddu ealle   bliðu mode
þæt me beo Matheus helm,   Marcus byrne,
leoht, lifes rof,   Lucos min swurd,
scearp and scirecg,   scyld Iohannes,
30   wuldre gewlitegod   wælgar Serafhin.
    Forð ic gefare,   frind ic gemete,
eall engla blæd,   eadiges lare.
Bidde ic nu sigeres god   godes miltse,
siðfæt godne,   smylte and lihte
35   windas on waroþum.   Windas gefran,
circinde wæter   simble gehælede

11. A Journey Charm

I encircle myself with this rod and entrust myself to God's grace,
against the sore stitch, against the sore bite,
against the grim dread,
against the great fear that is loathsome to everyone,
5   and against all evil that enters the land.
A victory charm I sing, a victory rod I bear,
word-victory, work-victory. May they avail me;
that no mere obstruct me, nor foe oppress me,
nor my life turn to terror,
10   but save me, Almighty, Son and Holy Ghost,
Lord worthy of all glory,
as I have heard, heaven's Shaper.
Abraham and Isaac
and such men, Moses and Jacob,
15   and David and Joseph,
and Eve and Anna and Elizabeth,
Zacharias and also Mary, Christ's mother,
and also the brothers, Peter and Paul,
and also thousands of thy angels,
20   I call on to fend me against all fiends.
May they lead and guard me and protect my path,
wholly keep me and rule me,
guiding my works; to me the hope of glory,
the hand on my head, may the host of holy ones,
25   the company of conquering, righteous angels, be.
In blithe mood I bid them all
that Matthew be my helm, Mark my coat of mail,
strong light of my life, Luke my sword,
sharp and bright-edged, John my shield,
30   gloriously adorned, Seraph of the roads.
    Forth I fare; I shall find friends,
all the glory of angels, the lore of the blessed.
I pray now the God of victory, the mercy of God,
for a good journey, a calm and light
35   wind from these shores. I have heard of winds
rouse whirling waters. Ever secure

wið eallum feondum. Freond ic gemete wið,
þæt ic on þæs ælmihtgian frið   wunian mote,
belocun wið þam laþan,   se me lyfes eht,
40   on engla blæd   gestaþelod,
and inna halre hand   heofna rices,
þa hwile þe ic on þis life   wunian mote. Amen.

against all fiends, may I meet with friends,
that I may dwell in the peace of the Almighty,
protected from the evil one who seeks my life,
40   established in the glory of the angels,
and in the holy hand of the Mighty One of heaven,
whilst I may live in this life. Amen.

12. Against a Wen

Wenne, wenne, wenchichenne,
her nu scealt þu timbrien, ne nenne tun habben,
ac þu scealt north eonene to þan nihgan berhge,
þer þu hauest, ermig, enne broþer.
5   He þe sceal legge leaf et heafde.
Under fot wolues, under ueþer earnes,
under earnes clea, a þu geweornie.
Clinge þu alswa col on heorþe,
scring þu alswa scerne awage,
10   and weorne alswa weter on anbre.
Swa litel þu gewurþe alswa linsetcorn,

and miccli lesse alswa anes handwurmes hupeban, and alswa litel þu
gewurþe þet þu nawiht gewurþe.

12. Against a Wen

Wen, wen, little wen,
here thou shalt not build, nor have any abode,
but thou shalt fare north to the hill hard by,
where thou hast a brother in misery.
5   He shall lay a leaf at thy head.
Under wolf's paw, under eagle's wing,
under eagle's claw, ever mayst thou fade.
Shrivel as coal on the hearth,
shrink as dung on a wall,
10   waste away as water in a pail.
Become as little as a linseed grain,

and much less also than a hand-worm's hipbone, and also become so
little that thou become naught.

SELECT BIBLIOGRAPHY

1. BIBLIOGRAPHIES

Annual Bibliography of English Language and Literature (Cambridge, 1921–), s.v. Old English.
The Year's Work in English Studies (London, 1921–), s.v. Old English.
Ker, N R: *Catalogue of Manuscripts containing Anglo-Saxon* (Oxford, 1957).

2. COMPLETE TEXTS

Grein, C W M: *Bibliothek der angelsächsischen Poesie*, revd. R P Wulker, 3 vols. (Kassel, 1883–98).
Krapp, G P and Dobbie, E van K: *The Anglo-Saxon Poetic Records* (New York and London, 1931–54). ii. *The Vercelli Book*; iii. *The Exeter Book*; v. *The Beowulf Manuscript*; vi. *The Anglo-Saxon Minor Poems*.

3. TEXTS OF INDIVIDUAL POEMS

Beowulf nebst dem Finnsburg-Bruchstück, ed. F Holthausen (Heidelberg, 1905–6). 6th edn. of the text (1929) contains also *Waldere, Deor*, and *Widsith*.
Beowulf, with the Finnsburg Fragment, ed. A J Wyatt and R W Chambers (Cambridge, 1914; 2nd edn., 1936).
Beowulf and the Fight at Finnsburg, ed. F Klaeber, 3rd edn. (Boston, 1936).
Anglo-Saxon Charms, ed. F Grendon (New York, 1930).
Anglo-Saxon Magic, ed. G Storms (The Hague, 1948). All the *Charms* with translations.
Deor, ed. K Malone (London, 1933).
Gnomic Poetry in Anglo-Saxon, ed. B C Williams (New York, 1914).
Runic and Heroic Poems of the Old Teutonic Peoples, ed. B Dickins (Cambridge, 1915). Contains *Waldere, Finnsburg Fragment*, and *Deor*.
Waldere, ed. F Norman (London, 1933).

Widsith: A Study in Old English Heroic Legend, ed. R W Chambers (Cambridge, 1912).
Widsith, ed. K Malone (London, 1936).
Widsith, ed. K Malone (Copenhagen, 1963). An expansion and revision of the preceding edition.

4. TRANSLATIONS

(a) General collections

Bradley, S A J: *Anglo-Saxon Poetry* (London, 1982). In prose. Contains *Beowulf,Widsith, Waldere, Deor, Wulf and Eadwacer, Maxims I* and *II, The Battle offinnsburh,* and selected *Charms.*

Cook, A S and Tinker, C B: *Select Translations from Old English Poetry* (revd. edn., Cambridge, Mass., 1926). In prose and verse. Contains selections from *Beowulf, Charms,* and *Gnomic Verses.*

Faust, C and Thompson, S: *Old English Poems* (Chicago and New York, 1918). In alliterative verse. Contains *Widsith, Deor, Waldere, Finnsburg,* selected *Charms,* and *Gnomic Verse.*

Gordon, R K: Anglo-Saxon Poetry (London, 1962). In prose. Contains *Beowulf, Finnesburgh, Waldhere, Widsith, Deor, Wulf and Eadwacer,* and *Gnomic Poetry.*

Kemble, J M: *The Poetry of the Codex Vercellensis.* With an English translation (London, 1843–56).

Mackie, W S: *The Exeter Book,* Part II (London, 1934). A text and verse translation of each of the poems in the latter half of the Exeter Manuscript.

Malone, K: *Ten Old English Poems* (Baltimore, 1941). In alliterative verse. Contains *Wulf and Eadwacer, Finnsburg, Widsith,* and *Deor.*

Rodrigues, L J: *Seven Anglo-Saxon Elegies* (Llanerch, 1991). Contains text and verse translations of *Deor* and *Wulf and Eadwacer.*

Spaeth, J D: *Old English Poetry* (Princeton, 1922). In alliterative verse. Contains *Beowulf, Widsith,* selected *Charms* and *Gnomic Verses.*

Thorpe, B: *Codex Exoniensis.* A collection of Anglo-Saxon Poetry from a manuscript in the library of the Dean and Chapter of Exeter. Complete text with translation (London, 1842).

(b) Individual works

Beowulf and The Fight at Finnsburg, J C R Hall (London, 1901). In prose. New edition (*Beowulf and the Finnsburg Fragment*) revd. C L Wrenn and J R R Tolkien (London, 1940).

Beowulf and the Finnesburh Fragment, C G Child (Boston, 1904). In prose.

The Oldest English Epic, F B Gummere (New York, 1909). In alliterative verse. Contains *Beowulf, Finnsburg, Waldere, Deor, Widsith*, and the German *Hildebrandslied*.

The Song of Beowulf, R K Gordon (New York, 1923). In prose. Included in Gordon's *Anglo-Saxon Poetry* (London, 1926).

Beowulf, W E Leonard (New York, 1923). In metre imitating the Nibelungen couplet.

Beowulf, A Strong (London, 1925). In the long ryhmed couplets used by William Morris in *Sigurd the Volsung*.

Beowulf, C W Kennedy (New York, 1940). In alliterative verse.

Beowulf, E Morgan (Kent, 1952). In verse.

Beowulf, E T Donaldson (London, 1967). In prose.

Beowulf, R P M Lehmann (Austin, Texas, 1988). In alliterative verse.

Widsith, R W Chambers (Cambridge, 1912). Text with translation.

5. CRITICAL STUDIES

Beowulf and its Analogues, ed. and trans. G N Garmonsway and J Simpson (London and New York, 1968).

Bonjour, A: *The Digressions in Beowulf* (Oxford, 1950).

Earle, J: *Anglo-Saxon Literature* (London, 1884).

Kennedy, C W: *The Earliest English Poetry* (Princeton, 1943). Reprinted (London, 1971).

Ker, W P: *Epic and Romance* (London, 1896).

Lawrence, W W: *Beowulf and Epic Tradition* (Cambridge, 1928).

Malone, K: 'Two English *Frauenlieder*', in *Studies in Old English Literature in Honor of Arthur G. Brodeur* (University of Oregon Press, 1963), pp. 106-28. A study of *Wulf and Eadwacer*.

Shippey, T A: *Old English Verse* (London, 1972).

Tolkien, J R R: *Finn and Hengest*, ed. A Bliss (London, 1982).

Anglo-Saxon Verse Charms, Maxims and Heroic Legends

Wardale, E E: *Chapters on Old English Literature* (London, 1935).
Williams, M: *Word-Hoard* (New York, 1940).
Williams, R A: *The Finn Episode in Beowulf* (Cambridge, 1924).
Wrenn, C L: *A Study of Old English Literature* (London, 1967).

6. HISTORY AND CULTURE

Aberg, N: *The Anglo-Saxons in England during the Early Centuries after the Invasion* (Uppsala, 1926).
Anderson, L H: *The Anglo-Saxon Scop* (Toronto, 1903).
Blair, P H: *An Introduction to Anglo-Saxon England* (Cambridge, 1956).
Chadwick, H M: *The Origin of the English Nation* (Cambridge, 1907).
Chambers, R W: *England before the Norman Conquest* (London, 1928).
Gummere, F B: *Germanic Origins* (New York, 1892), reissued as *Founders of England*, with supplementary notes by F P Magoun (New York, 1930).
Jiriczek, O L : *Northern Hero Legends*, trans. M B Smith (London, 1902).
Levison, W: *England and the Continent in the Eighth Century* (Oxford, 1946).
Olrik, A: *The Heroic Legends of Denmark*, trans. and revd. L M Hollander (New York, 1919).
Oman, C: *England before the Norman Conquest* (London, 1910).
Stenton, Sir F W: *Anglo-Saxon England*, 2nd edn. (Oxford, 1923).
Whitelock, D: *The Beginnings of English Society*, Pelican History of England, II (Baltimore and London, 1952).

166

The Author

Louis Rodrigues, poet, technical and literary translator, and lexicographer, was educated at the Universities of Madras, London (King's), Cambridge (Trinity Hall) and Barcelona and holds a doctorate in Anglo-Saxon. He writes mainly in English and translates from Spanish, Catalan and Galician. His work has appeared in literary journals in the UK, USA, Canada and Spain and his published titles include *A Long Time Waiting*, *Chiaroscuro*, *Anglo-Saxon Riddles*, *Seven Anglo-Saxon Elegies*, *The Battles of Maldon and Brunanburh*, and *Anglo-Saxon Verse Runes*. Jointly with his wife Josefina Bernet, he has published *Short Story Translation – from theory to practice* and four bilingual Spanish-English titles: *A Glossary of Commercial and Industrial Terms*, *A Dictionary of Idioms*, *Study Aids Synonyms* and *Study Aids Idioms* and is in the process of completing *A Dictionary of Synonyms*. He was one of the chief collaborators in the recently published *Collins Spanish Dictionary* (Third Version). Three of his verse translations from the Catalan are to be published later this year: *A Choice of Salvador Espriu's Verse*, *The Bullskin* (Salvador Espriu's *La Pell de Brau*), and *The Strangled Voice* (a selection from the work of five Catalan poets) as is *Go on, Laugh!*, his first novel.

Wordcraft
Concise English/Old English Dictionary and Thesaurus
Stephen Pollington

This book provides Old English equivalents to the commoner modern words in both dictionary and thesaurus formats.

Previously the lack of an accessible guide to vocabulary deterred many would-be students of Old English. Now this book combines the core of indispensable words relating to everyday life with a selection of terms connected with society, culture, technology, religion, perception, emotion and expression to encompass all aspects of Anglo-Saxon experience.

The Thesaurus presents vocabulary relevant to a wide range of individual topics in alphabetical lists, thus making it easily accessible to those with specific areas of interest. Each thematic listing is encoded for cross-reference from the Dictionary. The two sections will be of invaluable assistance to students of the language, as well as to those with either a general or a specific interest in the Anglo-Saxon period.

UK £9·95 net   ISBN 1–898281–02–5   240pp

Spellcraft
Old English Heroic Legends
Kathleen Herbert

The author has taken the skeletons of ancient Germanic legends about great kings, queens and heroes, and put flesh on them. Kathleen Herbert's extensive knowledge of the period is reflected in the wealth of detail she brings to these tales of adventure, passion, bloodshed and magic.

The book is in two parts. First are the stories that originate deep in the past, yet because they have not been hackneyed, they are still strange and enchanting. After that there is a selection of the source material, with information about where it can be found and some discussion about how it can be used. The purpose of the work is to bring pleasure to those studying Old English literature and, more importantly, to bring to the attention of a wider public the wealth of material that has yet to be tapped by modern writers, composers and artists.

Kathleen Herbert is the author of a trilogy, set in sixth century Britain, that includes a winner of the Georgette Heyer prize for an outstanding historical novel.

UK £6·95 net   ISBN 0–9516209–9–1   288pp

Looking for the Lost Gods of England

Kathleen Herbert

Kathleen Herbert sifts through the royal genealogies, charms, verse and other sources to find clues to the names and attributes of the Gods and Goddesses of the early English. The earliest account of English heathen practices reveals that they worshipped the Earth Mother and called her Nerthus. The names Tiw, Woden, Thunor, and Frig have been preserved in place names and in the names given to days of the week. The tales, beliefs and traditions of that time are still with us and able to stir our minds and imaginations; they have played a part in giving us *A Midsummer Night's Dream* and the *Lord of the Rings*.

Kathleen Herbert is the author of a trilogy, set in sixth-century Britain, that includes a winner of the Georgette Heyer prize for an outstanding historical novel.

UK £6·95 net ISBN 1–898281–04–1 176pp

A Handbook of Anglo-Saxon Food: Processing and Consumption

Ann Hagen

For the first time information from various sources has been brought together in order to build up a picture of how food was grown, conserved, prepared and eaten during the period from the beginning of the 5th century to the 11th century. No specialist knowledge of the Anglo-Saxon period or language is needed, and many people will find it fascinating for the views it gives of an important aspect of Anglo-Saxon life and culture. In addition to Anglo-Saxon England the Celtic west of Britain is also covered.

UK £7·95 net ISBN 0–9516209–8–3 192pp

The Battle of Maldon: Text and Translation

Translated and edited by Bill Griffiths

The Battle of Maldon was fought between the men of Essex and the Vikings in AD 991. The action was captured in an Anglo-Saxon poem whose vividness and heroic spirit has fascinated readers and scholars for generations. *The Battle of Maldon* includes the source text; edited text; parallel literal translation; verse translation; review of 103 books and articles.

UK £6·95 net ISBN 0–9516209–0–8 96pp

Beowulf: Text and Translation

Translated by John Porter

The verse in which the story unfolds is, by common consent, the finest writing surviving in Old English, a text that all students of the language and many general readers will want to tackle in the original form. To aid understanding of the Old English, a literal word-by-word translation by John Porter is printed opposite an edited text and provides a practical key to this Anglo-Saxon masterpiece.

UK £7·95 net ISBN 0–9516209–2–4 192pp

Alfred's Metres of Boethius

Edited by Bill Griffiths

In this new edition of the Old English *Metres of Boethius*, clarity of text, informative notes and a helpful glossary have been a priority, for this is one of the most approachable of Old English verse texts, lucid and delightful; its relative neglect by specialists will mean this text will come as a new experience to many practised students of the language; while its clear, expositional verse style makes it an ideal starting point for all amateurs of the period.

In these poems, King Alfred re-built the Latin verses from Boethius' *De Consolatione Philosophiae* ("On the Consolation of Philosophy") into new alliterative poems, via an Old English prose intermediary. The stirring images and stories of Boethius' original are retained - streams, legends, animals, volcanoes - and developed for an Anglo-Saxon audience to include the Gothic invasion of Italy (Metre 1), the figure of Welland the Smith (Metre 10), and the hugely disconcerting image of Death's hunt for mankind (Metre 27). The text is in effect a compendium of late classical science and philosophy, tackling serious issues like the working of the universe, the nature of the soul, the morality of power - but presented in so clear and lively a manner as to make it as challenging today as it was in those surprisingly Un-Dark Ages.

UK £14·95 net ISBN 1–898281–03–3 B5 212pp

Anglo-Saxon Runes
John. M. Kemble

Kemble's essay *On Anglo-Saxon Runes* first appeared in the journal *Archaeologia* for 1840; it draws on the work of Wilhelm Grimm, but breaks new ground for Anglo-Saxon studies in his survey of the Ruthwell Cross and the Cynewulf poems. It is an expression both of his own indomitable spirit and of the fascination and mystery of the Runes themselves, making one of the most attractive introductions to the topic.

For this edition, new notes have been supplied, which include translations of Latin and Old English material quoted in the text, to make this key work in the study of runes more accessible to the general reader.

UK £6·95 net ISBN 0–9516209–1–6 80pp

Monasteriales Indicia
The Anglo-Saxon Monastic Sign Language
Edited with notes and translation by
Debby Banham

The *Monasteriales Indicia* is one of very few texts which let us see how life was really lived in monasteries in the early Middle Ages. Written in Old English and preserved in a manuscript of the mid-eleventh century, it consists of 127 signs used by Anglo-Saxon monks during the times when the Benedictine Rule forbade them to speak. These indicate the foods the monks ate, the clothes they wore, and the books they used in church and chapter, as well as the tools they used in their daily life, and persons they might meet both in the monastery and outside. The text is printed here with a parallel translation. The introduction gives a summary of the background, both historical and textual, as well as a brief look at the later evidence for monastic sign language in England. Extensive notes provide the reader with details of textual relationships, explore problems of interpretation, and set out the historical implications of the text.

UK £6·95 net ISBN 0–9516209–4–0 96pp

The Service of Prime from the
Old English Benedictine Office
Text and Translation - Prepared by Bill Griffiths

The Old English Benedictine Office was a series of monastic daily services compiled in the late tenth or early eleventh centuries from the material that had largely already been translated from Latin into Old English.

UK £2·50 net ISBN0–9516209–3–2 40pp

Anglo-Saxon Runes

Tony Linsell

Books about runes tend towards the academic or the occult. This book bridges that gap and aims to help the reader understand how runes were used, and what meaning they had, for the people who used them. It also provides an insight into their values and how they perceived the world and their place in it.

Here the rune card illustrations are shown, one to a page, facing the appropriate verse from the Anglo-Saxon Rune Poem......this beautifully produced hardback book is well worth buying for this section alone which occupies just under half its 136 pages.....The remainder of the book makes fascinating reading and is full of – to me – unknown and interesting facts.....is a thoroughly enjoyable read as well as a delightful collection of evocative illustrations by Brian Partridge. Highly recommended.   Prediction Magazine

....Having read much about the Celtic influences on British life, I found it really interesting to learn something about the English history of these isles, and I actually found the general social and religious/magical background even more interesting than the runes and their meanings.....   Pagan Voice

UK £14·95 net   ISBN 0–9516209–6–7   Hardback 21cm x 27cm 144pp

---

Rune Cards

Tony Linsell and Brian Partridge

This package provides all that is needed for anyone to learn how to read runes.

This boxed set of 30 cards contains some of the most beautiful and descriptive black and white line drawings that I have ever seen on this subject.   ..Pagan News

These are fantastic....Real magic, fabulous and brooding imagery, and an easy doorway to runic realms....   Occult Observer

There is a thick little book which includes clear and concise instructions on how to cast the runes. It is detailed without being overbearing and Mr Linsell obviously knows his stuff.....

   Clamavi

The illustrations on the cards include prompts that will quickly enable the user to read the runes without referring to the book.

UK £12·95 net   ISBN 0–9516209–7–5   30 cards + booklet

For a full list of publications including our new series of booklets send a s.a.e. to:

Anglo-Saxon Books
25 Malpas Drive, Pinner, Middlesex. HA5 1DQ England
Tel: 081-868 1564

Most Titles are Available in North America from:
Paul & Company Publishers Consortium Inc.
c/o PCS Data Processing Inc., 360 West 31 St., New York, NY 10001
Tel: (212) 564-3730 ext. 264

Þa Engliscan Gesiðas

Þa Engliscan Gesiðas (The English Companions) is a historical and cultural society exclusively devoted to Anglo-Saxon history. Its aims are to bridge the gap between scholars and non-experts, and to bring together all those with an interest in the Anglo-Saxon period, its language, culture and traditions, so as to promote a wider interest in, and knowledge of all things Anglo-Saxon. The Fellowship publishes a journal, *Wiðowinde*, which helps members to keep in touch with current thinking on topics from art and archaeology to heathenism and Early English Christianity. The Fellowship enables like-minded people to keep in contact by publicising conferences, courses and meetings that might be of interest to its members. A correspondence course in Old English is also available.

For further details write to:
The Membership Secretary, Þa Engliscan Gesiðas
BM Box 4336, London, WC1N 3XX England.

Regia Anglorum

Regia Anglorum is a society that was founded to accurately re-create the life of the British people as it was around the time of the Norman Conquest. Our work has a strong educational slant and we consider authenticity to be of prime importance. We prefer, where possible, to work from archaeological materials and are extremely cautious regarding such things as the interpretation of styles depicted in manuscripts. Approximately twenty-five per cent of our membership, of over 500 people, are archaeologists or historians.

The Society has a large working Living History Exhibit, teaching and exhibiting more than twenty crafts in an authentic environment. We own a forty foot wooden ship replica of a type that would have been a common sight in Northern European waters around the turn of the first millennium AD. Battle re-enactment is another aspect of our activities, often involving 200 or more warriors.

For further information contact:
K. J. Siddorn, 9 Durleigh Close, Headley Park,
Bristol BS13 7NQ, England.

West Stow Anglo-Saxon Village

An early Anglo-Saxon Settlement reconstructed on the site where it was excavated consisting of timber and thatch hall, houses and workshop. Open all year 10a.m. – 4.15p.m. (except Yule). Free taped guides. Special provision for school parties. A teachers' resource pack is available. Costumed events are held at weekends, especially Easter Sunday and August Bank Holiday Monday. Craft courses are organised.

Details available from:
The Visitor Centre, West Stow Country Park
Icklingham Road, West Stow
Bury St Edmunds, Suffolk IP28 6HG
Tel: 0284 728718

The International Society
of Anglo-Saxonists

The International Society of Anglo-Saxonists (ISAS) is an organization open to all persons interested in any aspect of the culture of Anglo-Saxon England. ISAS intends to provide scholars interested in the languages, literatures, arts, history, and material culture of *Anglo-Saxon England* with support in their research and to encourage exchanges of ideas and materials within and between disciplines. All of this is accomplished primarily through biennial meetings of the Society during which members present papers and discuss topics of mutual interest. Many of the papers appear in a revised form in *Anglo-Saxon England*.

Benefits of membership include discount subscriptions to *Anglo-Saxon England* and other publications. Only members of the Society can attend and present papers at its meetings.

To join ISAS contact:

Patrick W. Conner, ISAS, Dept. of English, 231 Stansbury Hall,
West Virginia University, Morgantown, WV26506, USA.

Old English Newsletter

The *OEN* is a journal produced by, and for, scholars of Old English. It is a refereed periodical. Solicited and unsolicited manuscripts (except for independent reports and news items) are reviewed by specialists in anonymous reports. Four issues are published each (American) academic year for the Old English Division of the Modern Language Association by the Centre for Medieval and Early Renaissance Studies at the State University of New York at Binghamton.

General correspondence should be addressed to the Editor:

Paul E. Szarmach, CEMERS; SUNY-Binghamton,
PO Box 6000, Binghamton,
New York 13902-6000, USA.